Y0-BRL-447

LANGUAGE

LANGUAGE

A *Theory of Its Structure and Use*

Per Saugstad

Solum Forlag A/S. Oslo 1989
Humanities Press International Inc. New Jersey

First published in 1989 in Norway by SOLUM FORLAG A.S
and in the U.S.A. by HUMANITIES PRESS INTERNATIONAL,
INC., Atlantic Highlands, NJ 07716.

Library of Congress Cataloging-in-Publication Data

Saugstad, Per.
Language: a theory of its structure and use / Per Saugstad.
156 pp.
Bibliography: p. 143
Includes index.
ISBN 0-391-05 646-7

1. Language and languages. I. Title.

P 106. S 227 1989
400- -dc 19 88-38260
CIP

ISBN 82-560-0 552-1 (Solum)

Published with a grant from the Norwegian Council for Science and the Humanities.

To Randi

Contents

Foreword by Dell Hymes IX
Author's Preface 1
Introduction 5

Chapter 1

The state of the art 7
The historical-comparative study of language 8
Linguistics 9
Contributions of linguistics 14
Limitations of linguistics 17

Chapter 1

The state of the art (continued) 23
Cultural anthropology and language. 23
Psychology and language 25
Treatment of problems of language within physiology and biology 33
Conclusion 41

Chapter 2

Language is an expression of thoughts. 43
Thinking and language in the perspective of biological evolution 46
Terminological discussion 50
How does language affect thinking? 54
Conclusion 55

Chapter 3

Use of language is behaviour 57
The roots of language 59
The many uses of language. 63
Conclusion 65

Chapter 4

Plan for the scientific study of language 67
Positivist conceptions of science 68
An alternative to positivism 72
Procedure 77

Chapter 5

Categorization and the structure of knowledge. 83
The particular and the universal in perception and thinking 86
The structure of perception 86
Comment on the nature of the particular and the universal 90
The structure of knowledge 94
On the nature of concepts 97

Chapter 6

The structure of language 101
How words derive their meanings 102
Common names 103
Proper names 105
Conclusion 106
Objections to the belief that words are names 107
The structure of language 110

Chapter 7

Use of language. 113
The goals of the speaker and the listener 113
Knowledge may be more or less available 115
The performance of the speaker and the listener 117
The sentence is the unit of information 120
On the nature of grammar 124
Use of language is a skill 127

Chapter 8

The model and linguistic reality 129
Summary and evaluation of the model 130
Phylogenetic development of language 133
Ontogenetic development 136

List of references 143

Index of Authors 151

Index of subjects 155

Foreword

Dell Hymes

Per Saugstad looks at the bustling world of linguistics and reports a lack of progress. To a linguist and anthropologist such as myself, barely able to remain aware of the names of the increasing number of journals, and quite unable to be conversant with all their contents, that is astonishing. With so much activity, must there not be advance?

Saugstad is doubtful. Cardinal assumptions of modern linguistics—that language is a (closed) system, that it can be studied autonomously—seem questionable to him. Indeed, he rejects them.

Such a view might be taken to be in concert with the steady extension of what are taken to be the limits of language (more accurately, the limits of linguistics) to include discourse, pragmatics, and the like. And indeed Saugstad maintains that structure and function are interdependent, and that language must be understood as both mental and behavioral. Yet his concern is not simply with the extension of the scope of linguistic study beyond grammar, beyond the sentence. He argues for a change in the conception of grammar itself. He radically doubts that the sentence can be the basis of analysis, and consciously revives de Saussure's focus on the word. Language is an assembly of words serving as an instrument for communication; grammatical relations and sentence characteristics are secondary. And he is concerned to extend the scope of linguistic theory 'behind' grammar, one might say, arguing that thinking is prior to language, and that a theory must consider thinking, must indeed consider the evolution of language within communities of beings whose communicative activity can be considered to have involved thinking, and, initially, words. And with this comes what are in effect a pair of conversational maxims, one for speaker and one for hearer (ch. 7).

All this is argued in terms of an articulated conception of the philosophy of science, reflectively and speculatively, from principles and judgments as to what makes sense. I can not but recall that thirty-odd years ago Noam Chomsky argued for a conception of the nature of grammatical analysis in terms of an articulated conception of the philosophy of science. Chomsky also, of course, provided not only a perspective but also a 'paradigm', in the sense of a model of work, a way of defining problems and solving them, a framework for a new kind of 'normal science'. It is doubtful if linguists can be persuaded of a new way of doing things except as it provides a way of writing linguistic papers. Yet within the diverse landscape of formal linguistics today there are lexical and word-based models, and Saugstad's focus on the word may make connection with them.

An anthropologist can only welcome a perspective in which the evolution of human behavior finds a natural and fundamental place, and considerations of the nature of communicative behavior generally. The epistemological realism that goes with this is welcome too, as is the emphasis on language as an assembly of verbal tools. Such a conception is essential to an adequate anthropological understanding of language in a specific community and of language as an aspect of human cultural diversification and evolution. There is an increasing amount of interesting work that explicitly or tacitly presupposes such a conception. (If I may mention my own 'slogan', a conception of studying verbal means and their meanings to those who use them). One can hope for increasing interaction between such work and theoretical reflection such as this book about the bases of linguistics. Much is being learned, and more will be learned, that can reinforce and inform a conception of language as an assembly of instruments (ch. 8).

In clearing the space in which to develop his views, Saugstad touches on a wide range of basic problems, setting some aside as not part of his theory and noting the lack of adequate conclusions with regard to others. Such openness to uncertainty is uncommon. Perhaps, however, it is especially appropriate to our present state of affairs. Literary critics, philosophers and some others argue in terms of 'language', pronouncing truths of human language ex cathedra, picking and choosing ideas, and sometimes data, with little or no concern for linguistics as a cumulative scientific sphere. Within linguistics the hegemony achieved by Chomsky's approach in the 1960s no longer holds. Those who develop his present model (government and binding) are numerous, but a good many alternative approaches to grammar are put forward and developed. Those who do so do not have a feeling of defending castles against an inexorable tide, but of building on surer ground. And, as said, work 'beyond (and within) the sentence' under the rubrics of 'discourse', 'ethnography of communication', 'ethnomethodology', 'pragmatics', 'psycholinguistics', 'semiotics', 'sociolinguistics' flourishes. The seed of 'autonomous linguistics', the study of linguistic form for its own sake, has flowered into a 'perfection' of definition and ideological justification in Chomsky's work, while around it plants of other description spread helter-skelter. For linguistics it is a time of encyclopedias and handbooks, works which no matter what their focus and editorial orientation, necessarily accomodate diversity. Perhaps this is a time when reflective works, attentive not only to first principles, but also to how language is described, attentive both to structure and use, may sow seeds of a novel integrative approach that some of us shall live to see.

Author's Preface

During the 19th century great progress was was made in the scientific study of language. In the 20th century there has been an enormous interest in linguistic problems among scientists as well as among philosophers. Yet in that century I do not believe that substantial progress has been achieved. I think there are two main reasons for this.

In their attempts at establishing linguistics as an autonomous branch of science, linguists conceived too narrowly of their study. While they tended to reject the belief of 19th century linguists that a scientific study of language had to be carried out along historical lines, they continued to conceive of language as an object divorced from the activities of the speaker and the listener. Ferdinand de Saussure drew a distinction between language conceived of as a social object and language as embodied in the activities of the speaker and the listener. This distinction was a convenient one and allowed research workers to concentrate effectively on a restricted range of problems. The distinction was widely accepted, and when Noam Chomsky at the end of the 1950s suggested a reorientation of the study he did not question the belief that language might be fruitfully conceived of as an object divorced from the activities of speakers and listeners. The structure and function of language are two aspects of the same phenomenon. Language has a certain structure because it has a certain function and it has a certain function because it has a certain structure. No innovation of the scientific study of language can be made as long as the idea is upheld that the problem of the structure of language can be studied divorced from the way human individuals perform when they use language.

The second reason why no substantial progress has been made in the 20th century study of language is that the study has been carried out with the inadequate and incomplete scientific procedures advocated by positivist thinkers. These procedures led research workers one-sidedly to concentrate on accurate observations and descriptions and to rely heavily on induction. The result has been that scientists investigating language have been clinging to the fact that members of linguistic communities are capable of identifying words, sentences, and elementary sounds in their speech, and have neglected the study of the role played by perception, thinking, and culture in use of language. The study of language has become a formal, descriptive one ending up in endless terminological discussions. During the last decades the positivist ideas have been subjected to devastating criticism, but this criticism does not yet seem to have appreciably affected the approaches taken to the scientific study of language.

During the last decades psychologists, physiologists, biologists, and cultural anthropologists have taken a greater interest in the study of linguistic problems and cooperation between them and linguists have resulted in new perspectives. However, so far few attempts seem to have been made at integrating the diverse approaches into a comprehensive theory which relates structure to function. The present work is an attempt to conceive of the structure and function of language within a single model.

In the construction of the model the most difficult problems have been to relate language to perception and thinking and to find a way of describing the relationship between the speaker and the listener. The study of these relationships leads into a variety of broad issues which at present can have no clear and definite solution. Still, theorists must examine these issues with a view to finding a plausible—and sometimes the most plausible—solution to them. The conclusions which a theorist arrives at will appear as more or less self-evident to large groups of research workers. However, as long as the conclusions are not self-evident to all groups they must be examined even if this examination represents a rather unexciting and tedious task.

The present project is an extension and elaboration of ideas presented in a previous work which was published under the title: *A Theory of Language and Understanding* (Oslo: Universitetsforlaget, 1980). Realizing that it was not sufficient just to point to the fact that positivist ideas of science are highly dubious, I have worked out an alternative to the positivist approach. Furthermore, in my previous work I mainly dealt with questions related to the use made of language in communication. I was less concerned with the structure of language and did not then realize that structure and function cannot be separated in treatments of language. As I have already mentioned, in the present work I have tried to conceive of structure and function within a single model. Still further, in the previous work I did not believe it was possible to distinguish between the concept and the class or category. In the present work I have accepted this distinction. Otherwise I have retained the central ideas of the previous work. Because I was also preoccupied with the problem of accounting for the nature of concepts in a book on the foundations of pyschology (*A Theory of Communication and Use of Language. Foundations for the Study of Psychology*. Oslo: Universitetsforlaget, 1977) I want to mention that in that book I tended to take the position that thinking and language were inseparable, and due to a regrettable error in my reasoning I arrived at the conclusion that a class or category might have only one member. Though also in that work I took the position—which I still think is a highly plausible one—that in perception the particular and the universal are inseparable.

Considerations of language as a biological phenomenon have led me to stress the close relationship between structure and function. In an attempt at relating my theoretical position to those of other scientists I discovered that in his treatment of the role language plays in culture, Dell Hymes had stressed that structure and function cannot be divorced. By viewing language in a wider cultural perspective it seems possible to supplement the approach I have taken. I am grateful that Dell Hymes has been willing to study the manuscript for the book and provide it with a preface which widens the perspective I have taken to the problems.

To finish my project I have needed much help and advice. I have been overwhelmed by the generosity many of my colleagues at the University of Oslo as well as scientists abroad have shown when I have requested their help. Unfortunately I can here only express my thanks to those who over a longer period of time have helped to clarify my thinking.

Fredrik Barth, Ethnographic Museum, Even Hovdhaugen and Rolf Theil Endresen, Institute of Linguistics, Arne Løvlie, Institute of Biology Arild Lian, Institute of Psychology, all five at the University of Oslo, and Arnold L. Glass, Department of Psychology, Rutgers University, USA, have helped me plan the present project. I am grateful for the help they have given me over a number of years. Barth and Hovdhaugen have also read and corrected various versions of the manuscript.

I also want to express my indebtedness to Kåre Elgmork, Kjell Døving, both at the Institute of Biology, University of Oslo, Sherwood S. Washburn, Department of Anthropology, University of California, Berkeley, and Peter Marler, Rockefeller University, Field Research Center, New York, for help on problems of biology and physiology; to Fredrik Otto Lindeman, Institute of Linguistics, University of Oslo, and William S.-Y. Wang, Department of Linguistics, University of California, Berkeley, for help with problems of linguistics, to Tore Helstrup and Kjell Raaheim, both at the Cognitive Institute at the University of Bergen, Leif Stinessen, Department of Psychology, University of Trondheim, Boris F. Lomov, Ludmila J. Antsiferova, Andrey W. Brushlinsky, all three at the Academy of Sciences, USSR, and my close friend Kaare Meidell Sundal, for help on problems of cognition, to Enok Palm, Institute of Mathematics and Matthias Kaiser, Institute of Philosophy, both at the University of Oslo, for help on problems of philosophy of science, and to Georg Henrik von Wright, the Finnish Academy, Helsinki, for help on a problem of reference and meaning. I am also indebted to Roar Glefjeld and Rune Dahl, collaborators on a project on language acquisition in children, for discussions of all the main problems in the theoretical model.

Introduction

The scientific study of language is today spread over a number of different disciplines. Linguistics, philology, cultural anthropology, sociology, logic, psychology, and physiology have all developed research traditions for dealing with specific types of linguistic problems. The specialization is a result of the historical development of the various branches of science, but it is also necessitated by the fact that the study of language raises so many different types of problems. No single scientist can master the knowledge and the techniques required for the handling of all types of linguistic problems. Still, while a specialization is necessary, it is also easy to understand that it is unfortunate that research is spread over so many disciplines. One obvious disadvantage is that it is difficult to determine what are the essential problems to solve. Each discipline will tend to have its specific preferences as to what these problems are. Secondly, in order to solve a specific problem it is frequently necessary to answer questions which are dealt with within several disciplines. This makes it difficult for scientists working within one specific discipline to solve problems adequately. Thirdly, the compartmentalization of research activities hinders scientists in having access to knowledge and research techniques available for the solution of their problems. To counteract unfortunate consequences of the specialization, scientists from different disciplines cooperate and during the last decades there has been an increasing tendency towards work of an interdisciplinary nature. This tendency has manifested itself in the establishment of new research areas, such as psycholinguistics, sociolinguistics and neurolinguistics. Interdisciplinary work is a step in the right direction, but it is not sufficient for an integration of linguistic research. To achieve an effective integration it is necessary to construct a comprehensive theory or model which may help scientists see the relationships between the diverse aspects of language. To my knowledge few—if any—attempts seem to be made in this direction and in this book I am going to present a comprehensive theory, a theoretical model, for the scientific study of language.

To achieve an integration of the study of language it is natural to begin with an examination of the approaches taken to linguistic problems within the diverse branches of empirical sciences. This examination must aim at understanding the conceptions underlying the approaches and at finding out what the approaches have produced of factual knowledge about language. In Chapter 1 I have undertaken this examination. When past and current conceptions of language are more closely examined it is revealed that they are heavily dependent upon the scientists' beliefs concerning the relationship between thinking and language. For this reason I have found it necessary in a specific chapter (Chapter 2) to discuss this relationship. As I hope to show, studies of the non-human primate species have produced knowledge of great importance for an understanding of the relationship between thinking and language. Another belief which has deeply affected the study of language is that its primary function is communication. While I think present evidence strongly supports this belief, some modern investigators have disputed it. Moreover, the belief that the primary function of language is communication raises the problem of whether language should be regarded as a mental or a behavioural problem. To deal with this problem it is necessary to discuss in what sense language can be conceived of as a form of behaviour. This discussion naturally leads into a treatment of the present status of behaviourism. In Chapter 3 I shall discuss in what sense language can be conceived of as communication and behaviour. In that chapter I shall also consider other functions which have been ascribed to language.

To develop a theoretical model which may help integrate linguistic research, a procedure is needed. In Chapter 4 I shall discuss problems in the philosophy of science and suggest a procedure for developing the model. At the present state of knowledge a comprehensive theory of language must necessarily contain a number of rather imprecise and tentative formulations. For this reason I have tried to specify the steps in the procedure in such a manner that other scientists can correct errors and inadequacies in my reasoning.

Having in the first four chapters dealt with conceptions of language and procedures for studying it, in Chapters 5, 6, and 7 I shall develop the theoretical model. In a final chapter, Chapter 8, I shall give a summary of what I regard as the main points in my approach. In that chapter I shall also consider how the model may account for what I regard as important facts about language, and shall discuss certain implications of the model for empirical research.

Chapter 1

The state of the art

Notwithstanding the admittedly practical necessity for most scientists to concentrate their efforts in special fields of research, science is, according to its aim of enlarging human understanding, essentially a unity.
Niels Bohr. Analysis and synthesis in science, 1938.

Language has properties which make it natural to regard the investigation of it as forming part of a number of different branches of empirical science. It has been shown to change over time and philologists have regarded the study of it as a historical discipline. Language is also a cultural phenomenon and cultural anthropologists and sociologists have included it in their studies. Further, language is a behavioural phenomenon and some psychologists have incorporated the study in a general science of behaviour. Other psychologists, believing that their subject matter should be conceived of in terms of conscious processes, treat linguistic problems as forming part of a general study of cognition. Still further, activities involving language have a basis in physiological processes and light can therefore be shed on the subject by a study of the physiological processes underlying it. Finally, mention should be made of the fact that evolutionary biology has made clear that language must have evolved in man's phylogenesis, and modern biologists regard the study of it as forming part of a general study of biology. In addition to being treated as forming part of the empirical branches of science mentioned, from the beginning of the 20th century a number of research workers have insisted that language has properties which make it natural to conceive of the study of it as an autonomous branch of science, a branch termed 'linguistics'. Concentration on the different properties I have mentioned have led to different approaches to the study of linguistic problems. I shall deal with the various approaches with a view to evaluating their contributions to a present and future study of language. Because linguistics arose as a study closely related to the earlier historical-comparative study of language, I shall deal with the contributions of the linguists not at the end of this chapter, but after I have considered the work of the philologists.

The historical-comparative study of language

The study of language has been an essential part of human intellectual activities for more than 2000 years and extensive descriptive analyses of languages as well as a theoretical framework for such analyses existed already in Antiquity. And yet within a modern scientific tradition the emergence of this study as science is usually connected with the methodological changes within the historical and comparative study of languages which started at the end of the 18th century and flourished in the 19th century. (Accounts of the history of the study of language are given by Even Hovdhaugen, 1982; John Lyons, 1981; R. H. Robins, 1979.)

An important event was the discovery, usually attributed to William Jones, that Sanskrit bore a relationship to Greek and Latin which could hardly be incidental. A plausible way of explaining this relationship was to assume that languages which seemed to be related to each other had a common origin. In this way the 19th century historical and comparative study of language arose. Victoria Fromkin and Robert Rodman (1983, p. 298) characterized the early research in this way:

> The nineteenth century historical and comparative linguists based their theories on the observation that there is a resemblance between certain languages, and that the *differences* amongst languages showing such resemblance are *systematic*; in particular, that there are regular sound correspondences. They also assumed that languages displaying systematic differences, no matter how slight in resemblance, had descended from a common source language—i.e. were genetically related.

The historical-comparative study of language was concentrated on the Indo-European languages. Still it should be noted that this study was not only applied to the Indo-European family of languages but early also to other families of languages (e.g. the Semitic languages and the Finno-Ugric languages) and was gradually extended to a number of families of languages from all parts of the world.

The scholars of the 19th century were able to describe a number of linguistic phenomena and to provide explanations for them. Hence, it was a sound scientific endeavour. Their explanations were given in the form of historical developments of language, and research workers of the 19th and the beginning of the 20th century held that a scientific study of language must be carried out along historical lines. Linguists, such as Hermann Paul (1880) and Otto Jespersen (1922), argued convincingly for the belief that in order to understand why languages manifested similarities and differences, research workers had to study the historical development of languages. The historical-comparative approach was limited by the fact that it had to be based on written texts and the material on which the conclusions were based was frequently fragmentary. Also, the range of languages studied was limited.

Linguistics

While the historical and comparative approach dominated linguistics in the 19th century, the beginning of the 20th century was characterized by a return to synchronic descriptive linguistics. In Europe this development started with Ferdinand de Saussure, while a similar and mainly independent development in the USA was headed by Franz Boas, Edward Sapir and Leonard Bloomfield. These linguists considered it legitimate to describe the structure of natural languages without regard to their historical development. Their aim was to construct a framework which allowed them to describe languages as they existed at particular moments in time. They tried to divorce these descriptions from the historical development of the languages described. However, while they opposed the idea that a scientific study of language must be carried on along historical lines, they continued to conceive of their study as a study of the *products* of speech. Naturally philologists studying written forms of language cannot deal with the physiological and psychological activities present in speakers and listeners. Nor can they study the relationship between the speaker and the listener. This forces philologists to concentrate on the products of speech. Like the philologists, the linguists of the 20th century also concentrated on the products of speech. In conceiving of the subject matter of their science as that of verbal utterances, they continued the tradition of the historical-comparative study of language. In this connection it is worth noting that pioneer linguists, such as Saussure, Sapir, Bloomfield and many others were trained as philologists.

Written languages can be studied in a cultural perspective and philologists have extensively done so. This aspect of the earlier tradition was taken care of by Boas, Sapir, Bloomfield, and many other American linguists who in their investigations of the Amerindian languages emphasized the close relationship between culture and language. Still as I mentioned above, they did not try to conceive of language in terms of the interaction between the speaker and the listener; also to them the study of language was the study of the products of speech, the study of verbal utterances. *It is thus an essential characteristic of linguistics that it concentrates on verbal utterances and treats language as an abstract entity divorced from the physiological and psychological activities of speakers and listeners.*

In their attempts at conceiving of language as an abstract entity, linguists came to rely heavily on the idea that language is a system. As stated by William Labov (1971, p. 447): "— — —. If one concept were to be named as central to linguistic theory and practice, it would be that of a 'system'. Therefore, to understand the approach taken to the study of language by the linguists, one must make an effort to understand their idea of language as representing a system. Actually, the idea that language is a system may be seen as an elaboration of ideas traceable back to the German Romantic scholars Johann Herder and Wilhelm von Humboldt. Because these two thinkers did not only—directly or indirectly—influence Saussure and Sapir, but also in the modern era Noam Chomsky and the generative grammarians, I shall briefly review some of the ideas of the two scholars mentioned.

In the latter half of the 18th century Herder attacked the view that language is an expression of thoughts, which had been the dominant view up to his time. He argued that thinking and language had a common origin and were inseparable. In line with this idea he announced that the outlook on the world which came to expression in a people's poetry and cultural activities was profoundly affected by the language spoken by the people. In the first half of the 19th century these ideas were further elaborated by Humboldt. He claimed that concepts cannot be formed without language. It is in the nature of language, he held, (Humboldt, 1964, p. 405), that thoughts and the production of sounds as well as hearing form a unity:

> Language is the organ which forms thoughts. The intellectual activity, which is through and through spiritual and internal, and which so to speak leaves no trace, becomes external and perceptible by means of the speech sound. This activity and language is, therefore, one and indivisible. However, this intellectual activity is necessarily bound to be connected with the speech sound. Otherwise thinking cannot achieve distinctness; the idea cannot become a concept.

According to Robins (ibid) Humboldt even held that the utterance of a single word presupposes the whole of language, language as a semantical and grammatical structure. In passing it should be noted that the thesis which is named after Benjamin Whorf (1956) that the thinking of an individual is dependent upon the particular structure of the language spoken by the individual, was an expression of a Humboldtian view of language.

The idea that language represents a whole, containing thoughts, words, sounds and grammatical rules, became central in the thinking of the linguists at the beginning of the 20th century. Saussure tried to give a coherent and consistent expression of this idea and is by many regarded as the founder of modern linguistics. It is natural to begin this examination by considering his ideas of language as a system. Unfortunately Saussure's ideas have only been preserved in the form of notes taken of his lectures in a course which he gave on general linguistics. He seems to have been unwilling to publish his ideas in the form he could have given them in the years before his death. (For a review of Saussure's life and work, see George Mounin, 1968; Jonathan Culler, 1976.)

Saussure conceived of language as a totality in much the same way as Humboldt, but on some important points he was more explicit. According to Saussure, language could be regarded as elements making up a system. What he referred to as the value of an element was determined by the relationship the element had to other elements in the system. An essential point in his approach was that he seems to have believed that the value of an element might be determined solely by its difference to the other elements of the system. In other words, what was important was that the elements differed from each other, that they were in contrast to each other (Saussure, ibid, p. 120):

> Everything that has been said up to this point boils down to this: in language there are only differences. Even more important: a difference generally implies positive terms between which the difference is set up; but in language there are only differences *without positive terms*. Whether we take the signified or the signifier, language has neither ideas nor sounds that existed before the linguistic system, but only conceptual and phonic differences that have issued from the system. The idea or phonic substance that a sign contains is of less importance than the other signs that surround it. Proof of this is that the value of a term may be modified without either its meaning or its sound being affected, solely because a neighboring term has been modified.

The stress on the fact that the elements were determined by the relationships they had to each other led him to state that language was form and not substance. In other words, the essential thing about language was that it represents a structure.

Saussure struggled to find a unit for his system. He rejected the belief that the 'grammatical sentence' was the unit. He pointed out that a characteristic of sentences was that they did not seem to resemble each other. On the other hand, he also found it difficult to accept that the 'word' was the unit because what appears as the same word may have different forms. For example, the French word for 'horse' has the singular form *cheval* and the plural form *chevaux*. He ended up suggesting that a defining characteristic of language was that it contained entities which were *not* clearly identifiable:

> Language then has the strange, striking characteristic of not having entities that are perceptible at the outset and yet of not permitting us to doubt that they exist and that their functioning constitutes it. Doubtless we have here a trait that distinguishes language from all other semiological institutions.

Saussure thought the word came closest to representing the unit of language.

He spoke of elements on a phonological, a grammatical and a semantical level. So apparently he accepted the traditional tripartite division of language into: 1. a vocabulary or lexicon, 2. a set of grammatical rules, and 3. a set of elementary sounds. Saussure seems to have conceived of the three types of elements as making up sub-systems of language. Together the three sub-systems formed a comprehensive system. It is important to note that it is possible to speak of language as a system on each of the three levels as well as of language taken as a totality, comprehending the three sub-systems.

As I have already mentioned, Saussure assumed that the meaning of the words, the lexical items, were solely determined by the relationships they had to each other. Hence, in line with the ideas of Humboldt *he held that words do not derive their meaning from a reference to objects or concepts having an extra-linguistic status*. He expressed his position to the problem of meaning by stating that the sign did not stand for something else, but was composed of two inseparable parts, the sound image and the concept. The relationship between the sound image and the concept was likened to the two sides of a sheet of paper.

Saussure attempted to draw a distinction between language as actually spoken by a group of human individuals and language as a social object common to the individuals of the group. He referred to the former idea by the term 'la parole' and to the latter by the term 'la langue'. 'La langue' was thus conceived of as an entity abstracted from the physiological, psychological, and cultural activities. It was actualized in the speech of the individual and thus only potentially present in the individual. Saussure seems to have thought that the scientific study of language was essentially a study of 'la langue'. As John Lyons (1981, pp. 220—221) emphasized, in the Saussurean tradition the idea that a distinction can be drawn between 'la langue' (which Lyons referred to by the term 'language system') and 'la parole' has served as a basis for the claim that linguistics can be conceived of as an autonomous branch of science:

> However, in the Saussurean tradition it has usually been taken to imply that a language-system is a structure that can be abstracted, not only from the historical forces that have brought it into being, but also from the social matrix in which it operates and the psycho-

> logical process by which it is acquired and made available for use in language-behaviour. Thus interpreted, the Saussurean slogan, whether it originated with the master himself or not, has often been used to justify the principle of the *autonomy* of linguistics (i.e. its independence of other disciplines) — — —.

Actually, not only the followers of Saussure, but also linguists of most other persuasions seem to have accepted that language can be studied as an abstract entity separated from the activities of speakers and listeners.

In the 1950s the approach taken to the study of language by the linguists got an eloquent spokesman in Noam Chomsky. (1957, 1965, 1972, 1980). Like Saussure he made a distinction between language conceived of as an abstract entity and the activities involved in its production. He referred to the latter activities by the term 'performance'. Hence, the term 'performance' corresponds more or less to Saussure's term 'la parole'. However, Chomsky conceived of language as a system in a manner which differed from that of Saussure. Chomsky elaborated upon the old idea of a linguistic rule and conceived of language as a system of rules internalized by the speakers of a language. The speakers were said to have a knowledge of this system and this knowledge was referred to as the competence of the speakers of a language. Hence, the term 'performance' was contrasted to the term 'competence'. According to this way of looking at matters, the linguists trying to construct a model of language (referred to as a grammar of a language) might be said to propose a hypothesis concerning this internalized system (Chomsky, 1972, p. 26):

> The person who has acquired knowledge of a language has internalized a system of rules that relate sound and meaning in a particular way. The linguist constructing a grammar of a language is in effect proposing a hypothesis concerning this internalized system.

While Saussure was hesitant as to whether the sentence should be included in' la langue' (and may even have tended to think that it belonged to' la parole'), Chomsky made the sentence central in his conceptions of language. He defined language as "a set (finite or infinite) of sentences, each finite in length and constructed out of a finite set of elements". While, as I noted above, Saussure thought the word came closest to representing the unit of language, the word seems to have disappeared in Chomsky's conceptions of language. As emphasized by Lyons (1981), he did not go into the problem of how sentences or the elements of the sentences obtained their meaning, but restricted himself to saying that language was a pairing of sound and meaning. Nor did he go into the problem of making clear how the abstract notion of a sentence is related to concrete utterances. (On this point, see Lyons, ibid, p. 165.) Furthermore, in line with the tradition established by Bloomfield, he held that phonology and syntax could and should be studied without reference to semantics. (On this point, see Lyons, 1970.)

By making certain assumptions about the nature of grammar Chomsky and other contemporary linguists have developed models for describing the grammar of a particular language in which certain verbal utterances are seen as so- called transformations of other utterances. The so called transformational grammars apparently allow linguists to describe the grammar of a particular language in a more precise manner. In an attempt at generalizing his ideas about the description of a particular grammar to descriptions of grammars in general (grammars of all the languages of the world) Chomsky suggested that human individuals had an innate capacity for making utterances in the form of sentences. The idea of an innate capacity for language is, of course, not at all implausible. However, since human individuals start acquiring a particular language and not all the languages of the world, the idea of an innate capacity is a highly speculative one. Evidently the precision and rigour in the grammatical description of particular languages break down when Chomsky and other transformational grammarians try to describe what might be regarded as a grammar in general, a grammar representative of all languages of the world.

Contributions of linguistics

Linguists have described the vocabularies, phonologies, and grammars of a large number of languages. For a variety of practical reasons these descriptions of particular languages are of great importance. However, unless linguists are capable of arriving at characterizations which hold true for all languages, the scientific study of language would result merely in a more or less arbitrary classification of the languages spoken in the world. For this reason, even if, as complained by Derek Bickerton (1981), most linguists have been concerned with individual languages, the aim of linguistics has been to arrive at statements which pertain to all languages. In line with this aim *I shall regard as facts about language only beliefs which seem to be true of all languages.*

While linguists may disagree on how language may most appropriately be characterized, it seems to be widely accepted that in the speech of all peoples of the world it is possible to identify three types of elements: 1. elements in the form of sentences, 2. elements which have more or less definite meanings and which are combined into sentences, and 3. elements in the form of specific sounds which have no meaning apart from the meaning that must be ascribed to them as a consequence of the fact that they form part of speech. I shall comment on the three types of elements.

1. With regard to the first type of elements it should be noted that so far linguists have not been able to give an adequate definition of the term 'sentence'. However, they seem to have been able to show that in the speech of all people sentences are formed according to definite rules. While speakers produce many utterances which are not in the form of grammatical sentences, it is highly reasonable to argue that a large number of such utterances can be regarded as sentences which are not completed. Linguists have also presented good arguments that utterances in the imperative which in some languages may lack a subject (a noun phrase) as, for example, utterances, such as "Go", "Come" and "Wait", may be regarded as sentences. While there are utterances, such as the English "Help", "Water", and "Fire", which are not easily classifiable as sentences, *it may be regarded as a fact that speakers of all communities tend to make their utterances in the form of sentences.*

2. In the speech of all peoples of the world it seems possible to identify elements having definite meanings. Hence, while linguists may disagree as to how meaning is to be defined, it is a fact that elements of this type can be identified. However, it has proved to meet with great difficulties to describe in a simple and consistent manner the nature of this type of second elements. In addition to elements in the form of words, all languages contain elements which have a definite meaning, but which are not easily regarded as words. For example, in the English language there are elements of the types of inflectional endings, prefixes, suffixes, and intonation patterns which have meaning, but which are not regarded as words. Therefore, a description of speech in terms of words is incomplete. There is the further difficulty to be overcome that in describing language in terms of words, that the concept 'word' is an abstraction. The elements speakers of a language identify as words may have different forms. For example, speakers of English will tend to regard the forms: *sings*, *singing*, *sang*, and *sung* as forms of the verb *sing*. One may distinguish between the different forms of a word and the abstract concept 'word' by introducing a specific term for the latter concept. Some linguists use the term 'lexeme' for this latter concept, and when I use the term 'word' I shall use it in the meaning of a lexeme. However, even if the use of a specific term for the abstract concept may help to remove an ambiguity, it may still be considered unfortunate to describe language by means of a concept which is as abstract as that of a word.

Some of the difficulties met with in attempts at describing language in terms of words can be avoided by undertaking the description in terms of the smallest segments having a meaning, in terms of so-called 'morphemes', and many modern linguists prefer this way of describing languages.

However, a description in terms of morphemes also raises problems which are not easily handled. In the first place, it is sometimes not possible to point to a specific segment which represents a specific type of meaning. For example, the English word form *mice* denotes an animal of a certain kind, but it also denotes that reference is made to a plurality of animals of this kind. Apparently *one* single form of the word denotes both the kind of animal and the fact that a plurality of animals of the kind is meant. Another well known example is the past tense of English irregular verbs, such as *sang*. Here one single form of the word denotes not only a certain activity, but also that this acitivity is referred to as having taken place in the past. Another and more important objection to a description of language in terms of morphemes is, as shown by P. H. Matthews (1972), that some languages, such as Latin, seem to resist an analysis in terms of morphemes. (A review of some of the difficulties met with in undertaking a description of language either in terms of words or morphemes is found in Lyons, 1968, 1977, 1981; Fromkin and Rodman, ibid).

In connection with the difficulties mentioned with regard to attempts at describing languages in terms of morphemes, mention should be made of the fact that words and the other types of morphemes may not be of equal importance in speech. Words seem to be far more important than the other meaningful elements. In speaking one has the impression of manipulating words, but not other types of morphemes, and characteristically, when people learn a foreign language they initially concentrate on the words. Even if morphemes may be divided into lexical and grammatical ones, the term 'morpheme' may represent an unfortunate abstraction.

I think it must be concluded that neither a description of speech in terms of words nor a description in terms of morphemes is satisfactory. While I shall keep in mind the difficulties met with in attempts at characterizing the elements having definite meanings, I shall not take a stand on this issue until I have discussed how this type of elements obtains their meaning. I shall use the term 'linguistic sign' to refer to all types of discrete elements which have meaning in speech.

3. Linguists have found that the sounds making up the speech of the peoples of the world differ. However, they have been capable of showing that all languages have a relatively small number of sounds which make up the meaningful elements. They have also been able to show that the elementary sounds of the different languages, the so-called phonemes, are combined according to rules. Hence, while there are differences from language to language with regard to the third type of elements, all languages may be said to have the same type of phonological basis. This represents a third important fact about speech.

As I made clear in the first part of this chapter, students of language have for 200 years systematically searched for similarities between languages. However, apart from the three facts about language which I have discussed, they do not seem to have been able to find other features common to all languages of the world. Yet a finding by Joseph Greenberg (1963) gives some promise of revealing structural features which may be said to be universally true. Greenberg investigated the order in which the subject, the verb and the object of declarative sentences tended to appear. It turned out that only the following three out of the six possible orders tended to appear: VSO, SVO, and SOV. This finding shows, of course, that the syntactic structure of all languages of the world differ in one important respect. However, Greenberg made an ingenious use of his finding. He showed that when a language tended to have one of these orders, it also tended to have other orders between the various parts of speech. This latter finding suggests that certain grammatical relationships may be universal.

In addition to the facts about language I have discussed above, linguists have shown that in spite of the great differences in structure found among languages they all seem to be about equally effective as means of communication. This is probably an important fact about language. Also they have shown that over time the phonological basis, the grammar, and the vocabulary of languages undergo changes. This may represent another type of fact or facts about language.

Limitations of linguistics

Having discussed the main contributions of linguistics I shall examine the idea that language is a system and the claim that linguistics is an autonomous science.

Before I begin my examination of the idea that language is a system, I want to emphasize that I believe the Saussurean idea of treating the elementary sounds of language as a system has proved to be fruitful. This idea was further developed by Nikolai Trubetzkoy and Roman Jakobson and later by American linguists. The study of the phonological basis of language as a system of elementary sounds, phonology, has no doubt been a productive area of research. The area is closely related to phonetics and thus has a basis in acoustics and physiology. I think it is perfectly adequate to speak of a phonological system.

The structural approach has proved fruitful also in the study of grammar. By extending the range of languages Edward Sapir (1921) and Leonard Bloomfield (1933) were capable of giving new and interesting perspectives on problems of grammar. Also, by adhering more strictly to the definition which can be given of terms by considering the relationship grammatical elements have to each other, Zellig Harris (1951), Noam Chomsky (1957) and others have been capable of improving the rigour of the formulation of grammatical rules. (For a review of this work, see Lyons, 1968; Robbins, ibid.) However, it is one thing to show that a number of linguistic features can be better understood by a consideration of relationships between grammatical elements, quite another is to say that grammatical rules represent a system in the sense that changes in one rule necessarily affects the other rules. In the presentation of Saussure's ideas I noted that he believed that thinking and language were inseparable. If this belief is rejected and instead thinking and use of language are regarded as different and separable activities, it will be understood that it is possible to argue that utterances containing words which have not been related to each other by grammatical rules may be perfectly understandable in a great variety of situations. From this it seems to follow that grammatical rules cannot be regarded as necessary, unless it can be shown that thinking and language are inseparable. If grammatical rules are not necessary it may be possible to add or subtract a rule from a language without necessarily affecting the other grammatical rules. On this premise *it seems perfectly sensible to regard grammatical rules as linguistic conventions.* The fact that they are conventions does not, of course, make them unimportant. It will be noted that the fact that some rules seem to be more important than others and that they may be ordered in a hierarchical manner, does not show that they represent a system in the sense discussed here.

While the emphasis on relationships has proved useful in phonology and the study of grammar, it has hardly been shown to be useful in the study of semantics. The evidence which Saussure adduced for his idea that word meaning was determined solely by the relationships between the words of a language was meagre. His main point seems to have been that one does not find a complete correspondence between the meaning of words of different languages. For example, the meaning of the French verb *louer* (une maison) does not quite correspond to the German verb *mieten*. While the French word can mean both that one rents a house from another person and that one rents a house to another person, the German word has only the former meaning. To express the latter meaning German uses the verb *vermieten*. Another example given by Saussure is the difference in meaning between the French word *mouton* and the English word *sheep*. Whereas the French word can mean both the animal 'sheep' and a piece of meat taken from the corpse of the animal, the English language has one word for the animal (*sheep*) and one for the meat of the sheep (*mutton*).

Good reasons can be given for believing that the structuralist approach to the study of semantics is based on inadequate conceptions. Whatever positions one takes to the problem of accounting for the way words obtain their meaning, it is a fact that the meaning of a number of words corresponds fairly well to the way not only human individuals, but also individuals of the non-human primate species perceive the world. For example, individuals of the primate species do probably perceive objects such as rocks, stones, sand, water, trees, plants, animals, food, moving objects and activities engaged in by animals, such as eating, running, climbing in much the same way as human individuals. Apparently the meaning of a large variety of words seems to correspond to objects of perception, such as those mentioned. It is natural—as a number of philosophers and scientists have held—that words of this type obtain their meaning from a reference to objects and actions. Saussure's followers seem to have believed that decisive arguments had been presented *against* the belief that words—or in general linguistic signs—derive their meaning from a reference to extra-linguistic objects or concepts. The fact that the vocabularies of different languages do not correspond to each other is not a valid argument for Saussure's position. Suppose languages have a smaller number of signs and expressions than speakers have concepts, and further that depending upon cultural conditions human individuals designate by words different concepts, it follows that the vocabularies of different languages need not correspond to each other. The two assumptions I have made are clearly highly plausible. Hence, Saussure's argument is not a good one.

It should be noted that it is difficult to demonstrate by empirical research that the meaning of words can be accounted for by assuming that they form part of a system. If we assume that language has a basis in man's perception and thinking, and further, that man's perception and thinking have a definite structure, the relationships found between various types of words may simply reflect this structure and may not be a result of the position of the words in language as a system. As I shall show in later chapters, both these assumptions are highly plausible. Obviously it is difficult to conduct a study which allows one to control for the possibility that perception and thinking may be structured independently of language. (For reviews of studies of semantics based on the idea that words form part of a system or field, see Lyons, 1977; George Miller and Philip Johnson-Laird, 1976.)

If neither the items of the vocabulary nor the grammatical rules form systems in the Saussurean sense, it would be strange if the three sub-components of language taken together should form a system. An indication that they do not is found in the fact that even if a language borrows a number of words from another language, the phonology and grammar of the language may remain unaffected. In this connection it is of interest to note that in the English language the largest portion of the words are of Romance origin while the grammar has developed out of the earlier grammar of a Germanic language. William Labov (1971) has questioned the belief that the three sub-components represent a system. He pointed out that in the development of Creole languages the lexicon and the grammar can undergo substantial changes without affecting each other. Also, languages can be put together from highly diverse components and, still further, languages in close contact over long periods of time may become identical in some components, but different in others.

There can be no doubt that in part the popularity of Saussure's ideas was due to the fact that they were in agreement with an influential intellectual movement, namely structuralism. This movement stressed that in studying more complex human and social phenomena it was in general more advantageous to concentrate on relationships between events or phenomena than on properties of the events or phenomena. This is a metaphysical belief which is not easily evaluated and I shall make no attempts to do so. I shall restrict myself to pointing out that it is frequently difficult to decide whether what one studies should be regarded as a relation between two or more entities or as a property of the entities. Moreover, in many instances it is probably more fruitful to concentrate on properties of events than on relationships between them. It is hardly warranted to raise the central belief of structuralism to a methodological principle.

Whether the idea that an area or field of research can be fruitfully studied by conceiving of events or phenomena as forming part of a system depends upon the degree to which the area or the field can be delimited. If it is not possible to delimit a postulated field of research it is hardly an advantage to regard it as a system and to try to specify events and phenomena in terms of postulated internal relationships. Looking at matters in this way the idea that language represents a system can only be a fruitful one if language as a postulated field of research can be fairly well delimited. The question to be answered is accordingly: Is it possible to delimit language as a field of research in a clear and unambigious manner? I shall point to certain apparent difficulties in attempts at delimiting language as a field of research.

One difficulty concerns the relationship between thinking and language. Should thinking be included in the study of language? Due to the fact that we have inadequate knowledge about the relationships between thinking and language, it is difficult to answer this question. As I have already mentioned, Herder and Humboldt answered the question in the positive and so did Saussure and his followers. In contrast, a number of past, but also present thinkers have answered the question in the negative. Apparently the answer one gives to this question affects attitudes to a great number of issues in linguistic research. A second difficulty met with in delimiting language stems from the fact that language can be regarded both as an expression of thoughts (as a mental phenomenon) and as a form of behaviour. To delimit language as a field of research one will have to clarify these two attitudes to language. This leads into questions of the following type: Is language primarily a means of communication?

Is it an expression of emotions? Is it a means of thinking? These questions have no simple answers.

In a discussion of the idea that language is a system, mention must also be made of the fact that it is difficult to understand how language could originate in phylogenesis as a system. As regards the ontogenesis I think there is good evidence that language is not acquired as a system.

Having shown that the idea that language is a system meets with difficulties, I shall turn to the claim that linguistics is an autonomous science. Linguistics is based on the fact that in speech it is possible to identify the three types of elements discussed in the previous section (sentences, morphemes, and phonemes). If it is possible to study in a productive manner the relationships between these three types of elements without basing the study on assumptions about function or performance, linguistics may be regarded as an autonomous science.

I shall begin by considering the study of the relationship between the elementary sounds, the phonemes. There can be no doubt that by a study of the relationship between the elementary sounds as these are identifiable in speech, linguists have been able to shed light on the basis which speech has in the production of sounds. One might think that one has thereby documented that the study of phonology proves that linguistics can fruitfully be regarded as an autonomous science. This conclusion seems to be too rash. I think one can argue convincingly that the study of phonology has a necessary basis in knowledge about function. One can conceive of the study as carried out on the assumption that the function of the elementary sounds is to produce discrete, identifiable symbols, and that in terms of this overall idea it has been possible to investigate problems concerning relationships between the sounds. Viewed in this way *the progress made in phonology may be said to be a result of a combination of considerations concerning structure and considerations concerning function.*

I shall turn to the study of the relationships between the morphemes in the formation of sentences. As we all know, it is possible to identify a variety of different grammatical features or rules in the speech made in all languages, and grammars can be written for all languages. However, because at the present state of knowledge grammarians are not capable of stating what is meant by a sentence without referring to the relationships between the morphemes, there is no way to find out which of all the particular grammars represents the grammar of language. It must be noted that inductive procedures alone do not allow one to reach decisions on this point. Apparently what is lacking in the study of grammar is a conception of the sentence which allows one to say what is the nature of grammar. It is difficult to understand *how one might conceive of a sentence in a fruitful manner without stating what its function is in language.* One may, therefore, conclude that because the study of grammar has been separated from the study of function, it has remained unproductive. As I noted earlier in this chapter, Chomsky made no attempt to specify what he meant by a sentence and this failure I think made his attempts to account for grammar unproductive.

By way of conclusion I shall say that one cannot in a productive manner study the relationship between the elementary sounds, the morphemes and the sentences unless in this study one includes the study of the performances people make when they use language. In other words, *in a productive study structure and function must be seen in relation to each other*. If one accepts this conclusion linguistics should not be regarded as an autonomous science.

Before I leave the discussion of the question whether linguistics should be regarded as an autonomous science, I want the reader to note that to make the study of language more productive one cannot simply extend linguistics to include parts of other sciences, such as cultural anthropology, psychology, physiology, and biology. New conceptions of language are needed. Moreover, as I shall argue in Chapter 4, more adequate conceptions of scientific procedures are also needed.

Chapter 1

The state of the art (continued)

Cultural anthropology and language

Saussure stressed the social nature of language, but, as I have mentioned, he dealt with language only as a formal system abstracted from the use made of it in society. Cultural anthropologists have stressed the role played by language in society and the effect of culture upon language. A strong impetus to the study of the relationship between culture and language was given by Franz Boas and Edward Sapir, who made this relationship central in their investigations of the Amerindian peoples, and a number of cultural anthropologists have later shed light on a variety of linguistic problems by treating them in the framework of cultural anthropology.

The anthropological investigations of language represent an important extension of the studies undertaken by the linguists. Cultural anthropologists have emphasized that in order to understand the nature of language it is essential to understand the functions language has in society. As I pointed out previously in this chapter, the functional aspect of language has been almost entirely neglected in linguistics. In his *Foundations of Sociolinguistics* Dell Hymes (1974) has drawn attention to the fact that hesitations, interruptions, incompleteness and errors which occur in speech must frequently be understood in terms of the cultures to which the speakers belong. Further, to explain choice of words, specific ways of pronunciation and choice of various grammatical traits, it is necessary to view language as a cultural phenomenon. Still further, as emphasized by Hymes (ibid) and John Gumperz (1982), in order to participate in verbal discourse, an individual must be capable of using a number of clues which are specific to her/his culture. Such clues are the use of specific types of intonations, stress, gestures, and reference to specific types of facts of a cultural and historical nature. Speakers must have what Hymes (ibid) termed 'communicative competence'. As insisted by him (Hymes, ibid, 1947), "linguistics cannot claim to be a science of language without constituting itself on an adequate functional foundation".

The relationship between culture and language is extremely complicated and, as admitted by Hymes (ibid), cultural anthropology seems far from being able to give an adequate account of how language and culture are related to each other. In this connection mention should be made of the fact that rudiments of cultural activities have been found in populations of non-human primate species. (On this point, see Passingham, 1982.)

Further, mention should be made of the fact that, as argued persuasively by Richard Leakey (1982), in the evolution of man use of language did probably evolve after a number of other cultural activities had been established. Thus more recent biological and anthropological studies indicate that culture cannot one-sidedly be regarded as based upon language. Language must be viewed as only one of the roots of culture and *to get a deeper understanding of language an account must be given of how language and culture have interacted through man's earlier and later history.*

Research workers trained in the traditions of historical-comparative philology and linguistics have assumed that the study of language must take its point of departure in language conceived of as an abstract system manifested in verbal utterances. They will probably tend to agree with Ronald Langacker (1967, pp. 36—37) when he argued that "we must know what sort of thing a language is before we can hope to understand how the speaker and the hearer use it in practice". Hymes (ibid, p. 47) has questioned this belief and has argued that the point of departure for a study of language must be taken in the concept 'speech community':

> Speech community is a necessary, primary concept in that, if taken seriously, it postulates the unit of description as a social, rather than linguistic, entity. One starts with a social group and considers the entire organization of linguistic means within it, rather than start with some one partial, named organization of linguistic means, called a "language". This is vital because the notion of "a language" can carry with it a confusion of several notions and attributes that in fact have to be sorted out.

The point made by Hymes is important because it counteracts the tendency to conceive of the basis of language as the verbal utterance and focuses attention on the social and cultural origin of language. Yet it would be going to another extreme to insist that a study of language must take its point of departure in the speech community and not in an analysis of verbal utterances. Structure and function are inseparable. Because language has a certain structure it has a certain function (or certain functions) and because it has a certain function (functions) it has a certain structure. An adequate treatment of language must give due emphasis to both these aspects.

The emphasis in cultural anthropology on the social nature of language should not lead one to overlook that studies within this tradition have contributed also to making research workers more aware of the variability found in speech between members of the same speech community. Bloomfield (1927) has drawn attention to the variability in linguistic performance which can be found within what appears to be a very homogeneous speech community. Thus variability is found not only in large heterogenous speech communities, but also in smaller homogeneous groups. It should be noted that variability is restricted not only to vocabulary, pronunciation and grammar, but also reflects differences in the skill of using language. It is an important fact about language that considerable individual variations are found in formal structure as well as in use. Robbins Burling (1970, p. 196) noted that while speakers must conform to a number of social conventions they also introduce innovations:

> The forces for change and the forces for stability act upon language to put it into a state of slightly unstable equilibrium. On the one hand, the practical need for communication keeps it from changing too rapidly or at random. We must speak in ways that allow our listeners to understand us, otherwise language would become useless for most, though not quite all, of the uses to which it is put. At the same time our aesthetic pleasure in innovation puts pressure upon language for change, for we prize new words, new expressions, sometimes even new sounds. We admire the man who can rise above the restrictions of his language, who can bend it in new ways and avoid too familiar clichés. But freshness is the most perishable of qualities, and so the search for ever new expressions inevitably pushes the language further and further from its origins.

In connection with the point made by Burling it should be noted that the tendency in speakers to make innovations reveals that language cannot be accounted for only as a following of definite rules. This important point, to which I shall return in Chapter 7, is easily missed when language is treated as a formal system abstracted from the context in which it is used.

Psychology and language

When in the latter half of the 19th century psychology was established as an experimental science, language was not included among the topics studied. The pioneer empirical psychologists concentrated their study on problems of perception, memory, intelligence, and feeling, but did not extend their theories concerning these phenomena to problems of language. Wilhelm Wundt (1900, 1912), who was a central person in the etablishment of experimental psychology, took a great interest in psychology of language and made systematic and extensive studies of this topic. More recently Arthur Blumenthal (1970) has revived the interest in Wundt as the founder of psycholinguistics. Blumenthal has pointed out that in essential respects Wundt anticipated Chomsky. It is interesting to note that Wundt insisted that the study of language had to be based upon principles of psychology. Unfortunately his formulations of his psychological principles are so vague and diffuse that their value seems to be dubious and the philologist Hermann Paul (1920) could rightly oppose them. Paul based his approach on the psychology of Johann Friedrich Herbarth. Their disagreement probably did much to discredit a psychological study of language. Wundt was strongly influenced by Humboldt and held that thinking and language could not be separated, and that the sentence was the linguistic unit. He thought that he might account for the nature of the sentence in terms of his concept 'Gesamtauffassung', which was a central term in his psychological system. Wundt's treatment of many linguistic problems still deserves attention.

However, while Wundt's approach to psycholinguistics inspired many of his contemporaries this part of his work was rather quickly forgotten by the succeeding generations of psychologists. The reason was that Wundt thought the study of language could not be carried out by experimental methods. Language—like thinking—had to be investigated by a study of the history of culture, what Wundt termed 'Völkerpsychologie'. It was his experimental approach to psychological problems which attracted the interest of psychologists.

Like Wundt and his contemporaries, the next generation of European psychologists conceived of psychology as the study of consciousness. However, instead as the earlier generation had done, of assuming, that consciousness was built up by elements in the form of sensations and feelings, they conceived of consciousness as constituted by wholes or Gestalts. They extended the study to include also the study of thinking, but did not extend it to include problems of language.

While I think it is important to note that language was not included in the study of European experimental psychology, it should not be overlooked that from the beginning of the 20th century European child psychologists began systematic observations of the development of language. When in the 1920s Jean Piaget began publishing his influential work on the study of thought and language in the child there was already an extensive literature on language acquisition in the child. The interest in this topic has been a stable one from the beginning of the 20th century and up to the present. Also, even if few European experimental psychologists developed their framework so that they could deal with problems of language, there were European psychologists who in the first half of the 20th century took great interest in language. I have already mentioned Wilhelm Wundt. Another influential psychologist who worked extensively with problems of language was Karl Bühler (1934), who collaborated with Trubetzkoy and who constructed a comprehensive theory of language. Inspired by Saussure he concentrated on the linguistic sign and conceived of language as a system. By drawing upon Gestalt and field theoretical notions—as these came to expression in the European psychology of his day—he tried to account for the role played by the sign in verbal communication. (For reviews of Bühler's work on language, see Friedrich Kainz, 1960; Hans Hörmann, 1968.) In the USSR there was a remarkable interest in problems of language in the first half of the 20th century and some of the most creative research workers were trained in that country. In the previous section mention was made of Trubetzkoy and Roman Jakobson. Here I shall briefly account for the ideas of Lev S. Vygotsky (1962, 1981), who had a profound influence upon Soviet psychology, but whose work up to the 1960s remained unknown in the West. Influenced by Ernst Cassirer (1944) Vygotsky made the sign central not only in the study of language and thinking, but also in the study of man's social development. He gave an original turn to the old idea that the linguistic sign is a tool, arguing that in using linguistic signs man's consciousness was developed. By this use language became interiorized and verbal thinking arose. In contrast to Saussure and his contemporaries in the Prague School Vygotsky emphasized that language had a basis in perception and thinking and that perception and thinking could take place independently of language. Unfortunately Vygotsky does not seem to have been articulate about how language may become interiorized and thus how the linguistic sign as a tool can promote the development of man's consciousness.

Behaviourism, which dominated American psychology from the 1920s to the 1960s, brought a shift in conceptions of subject matter as well as in methodology. The main interest shifted from the study of perception, thinking, and feeling to that of learning. The leading behaviourists were theorists of learning. Neither Watson nor the main figures in behaviourist psychology in the 1930s and 1940s took a main interest in problems of language. However, in the 1950s influential theorists, such as Charles Osgood (1953), Burrhus Skinner (1957), O. Hobart Mowrer (1966) claimed that their theories of learning were capable of explaining linguistic performance. Under the editorship of Osgood and Thomas Sebeok (1954) a detailed program was elaborated for psycholinguistic research and the term 'psycholinguistics' was coined.

Prior to the advent of behaviourism scientists had been preoccupied one-sidedly with language as a mental phenomenon. Behaviourist psychologists must be credited for having drawn attention to the fact that language is also a behavioral phenomenon. Yet it is important to realize that *behaviourists have had very little to say about the performance of the speaker and the listener*. As pointed out by William Alston (1967), "it is a striking fact that behaviourally oriented theorists have generally managed to ignore the fact that the speaker is doing something when he speaks". Thus, for example, Skinner concentrated on the effect speaking had upon the speaker as a result of the fact that the listener reacted to the utterance. He had hardly anything to say about what the speaker had to do to transmit information to the listener. Also he had nothing to say about what the listener had to do to receive information.

The appeal which behaviourism had not only for psychologists, but also for philosophers, such as Charles Morris (1946) and William van Quine (1960), was probably mainly due to the fact that by taking a behaviourist approach it seemed possible to avoid the problem of meaning. This problem had been an embarrassing one in the earlier attempts at accounting for language. Apparently, if one could account for language in terms of physically describable stimuli and of motor responses, it seemed possible to avoid the problem of meaning. In addition to behaviourist psychologists and philosophers Bloomfield and the generation of linguists following him made great efforts to avoid making reference to meaning. (On this point in American linguistics, see Lyons, 1970). The slogan attributed to Wittgenstein; "Do not look for meaning, look for the use" characterizes the attitude of many philosophers in the middle of the 20th century. In America Nelson Goodman (1951) is, beside Quine, representative of this attitude. I shall make a few remarks on the behaviourist use of the term 'stimulus'.

Individuals of the mammalian species—and also individuals of species below this level—interact with the environment in a large variety of ways. As it is evidenced by the study of the history of the scientific study of perception, it is extremely difficult to determine what aspect of the environment, what type of physical energy, leads to a particular type of responses. Depending upon a number of factors which must be sought in the organism and not in the environment, the organism may react differently to what in terms of a physical description must be regarded as the *same* stimulation. Hence, when an organism emits a response this cannot be accounted for by reference *only* to the physically describable stimulation. The account must include factors which must be attributed to the organism. In other words, it is not possible to determine a stimulus without making an assumption about the orientation which the organism has to its environment at the moment of stimulation. As a result of this orientation the organism is capable of reacting to specific parts or aspects of the environment, of reacting selectively to different aspects of the physical energy surrounding it. Behaviourists have assumed that they are capable of accounting for this orientation by reference to the previous learning of the organism. However, as their critics have repeatedly pointed out, their claims that their theories can give this account is not warranted. Elsewhere (Saugstad, 1965, 1977) I have in detail discussed the difficulties which are inherent in the behaviourists' use of the terms 'stimulus' and 'response'. To give a coherent account of the organism's behaviour in terms of stimuli and responses, behaviourists have to make assumptions about meaning. *The claim that a behaviourist approach to problems of language allows scientists to avoid treating the problem of meaning is, therefore, not warranted.* It must be noted that the difficulties attached to the use of the term 'stimulus' are present also in the use made of the term 'information'. At the present state of development of the scientific study of perception and cognition it is not possible to define the latter term in a precise quantitative manner.

In connection with the point made about the use of the terms 'stimulus' and 'response' in attempts at avoiding the problem of meaning, mention should be made of the fact that attempts, such as made by Jon Barwise and John Perry (1983), to treat semantical problems by reference to the 'external situation' raise the same type of difficulties as those met with in treatments in terms of stimuli and responses. Because the same physical stimulation can give rise to different types of reactions, the term 'external situation' is ambiguous.

In his epoch-making criticism of the treatment made of linguistic problems by Skinner and the behaviourists, Chomsky (1959) rightly pointed out that they used the terms 'stimulus' and 'response' in an empty manner. Though, while the main points made by Chomsky were well taken, his criticism does, of course, not show that it is unfruitful to conceive of language as behaviour. It is a fact that in order to transmit information the speaker must perform or behave in a specific manner and, likewise, that in order to receive information the listener must behave in a specific manner. Also, it should be noted that not all behaviourists accepted the stimulus-response paradigm. Thus, for example, Edward Tolman (1932, 1948) was a stern critic of the way these terms were used. Tolman was one of my teachers of psychology and in Chapter 7 I shall show that his approach to the study of behaviour can be useful in the study of linguistic performance.

In the 1960s there was again a significant shift in conceptions of methodology and subject matter in psychology. The new, the so-called 'information processing approach', conceived of the mind in analogy with a computer. The subject matter was the mental representations individuals have when they accomplish tasks of various types. To account for these representations, psychologists working within this tradition proceed by postulating operations which are performed upon the information or knowledge available to the individual. By conceiving of the mental processes in terms of information and operations scientists can simulate the processes by means of electronic computers. This is, of course, an advantage in the new approach. Another strong point is that the requirement that an account of how a given task is accomplished shall be provided by reference to the knowledge available to the individual. This forces scientists to specify the previous learning necessary for the successful handling of the task. In European psychology of the first half of the 20th century this requirement was frequently left out of consideration. The psychologists tended to give merely a phenomenological description of how the subject conveived of the task. Also, in Piaget and psychologists inspired by him, this important point tended to be neglected. (For a review of work done in the information processing tradition, see Arnold Glass and Keith Holyoak, 1985; Robert Sternberg, 1981.) The apparent weakness of the information processing approach is that the use of terms, such as 'information', 'knowledge', 'operation', and 'representation' may easily come to entangle the scientist in subtle problems of consciousness.

Around 1960 a large number of American psychologists were tired of behaviourism and had returned to the older study of consciousness with fresh ideas. In this situation Chomsky's suggestion that language represented a system of internalized rules appealed to them and there was an explosive interest in the psychology of language. Psychologists— and also linguists—believed that the study of language might shed light on cognitive processes. This optimism was even shared by experienced research workers, such as Herbert Clark and Eve Clark (1976, p. 6), who believed that grammatical rules summarized facts of behaviour and, therefore, might help in the study of behaviour. They thought "grammatical rules should also take us a long way toward understanding the fundamental laws of thought and the nature of the human intellect". However, already at the end of the 1970s it had become clear to a number of cognitive scientists that the conception of linguistics as the study of a set of internalized rules is not easily transformed into a program of empirical research. In a commentary to the belief that neurophysiologists might profit from a study of this version of linguistics Roger Schanck (1979, p. 474) pointed out that the competence-performance distinction was ill-thought out and that in general this approach had very little useful knowledge to offer neuroscientists:

> At present, linguists have only the barest understanding of what is going on in language processing. Issues such as the interaction of knowledge in disambiguation, the nature of meaning, the role of inference in understanding, the application of high level knowledge structures for predictive understanding, the construction of sentence fragments prior to the completion of thought are only a very few of the language processing phenomena that are only beginning to be studied and can hardly be claimed to have provided much in the way of results .The whole problem of the interconnection of language and memory is not even remotely understood right now. What is it that neuroscientists are supposed to be learning from linguists? It cannot be much more than ill-formulated theoretical assessments of very low-level syntactic phenomena, the only kinds of phenomena that linguists have systematically studied.

As I have shown, during the history of psychology conceptions of subject matter have undergone a number of rather drastic changes. Psychologists have neither reached consensus as to how their field is to be delimited nor as to how sub-areas, such as perception, memory, and thinking are to be delimited. As a matter of fact, under the influence of positivist thinking, concern about the delimitation of the field and its sub-areas has not been regarded as important. As a result of the lacking consensus concerning the delimitation of the field it is difficult to relate to each other psychology and language.

It is easy to understand that the conceptions psychologists have of their subject matter will determine their beliefs about the relationship between psychology and language. The psychologists who conceive of their study as that of consciousness will have other beliefs about the relationship than those conceiving of it as behaviour. Also, different conceptions about the nature of consciousness will affect beliefs about this relationship. It should be noted that in whatever way psychologists conceive of psychology, they will have difficulties in stating in a clear manner how they conceive of the relationship between psychology and language. As I made clear earlier in this section, the term 'behaviour', as currently used by psychologists, must be elaborated to be useful in a scientific study of language. If psychology is conceived of as the study of consciousness, research workers are faced with the following difficulties. According to the Humboldtian-Saussurean view thinking is governed by language and must be regarded as forming part of language. Psychologists taking this position must regard language as forming an integral part of consciousness and hence of psychology. This makes it difficult to state what can be meant by the relationship between psychology and language. Psychologists who take the position that thinking and language are different capacities must in relating psychology to language give an account of thinking which does not invoke presuppositions about language. Elsewhere (Saugstad, 1977) I have treated in detail difficulties involved in the latter approach. I think it must be conceded that in whatever way one conceives of psychology, it is difficult to state what can be meant by psycholinguistics. To make the psychological study of language a productive one scientists must begin by clarifying the relationship between thinking and language and must also develop a conception of behaviour which allows them to conceive of language as behaviour.

As I pointed out in the discussion of linguistics, a main problem in this approach to the study of language is to decide whether or not language should be regarded as a system, and if it is to be so regarded, in what sense can it be said to represent a system. To deal adequately with this problem it is, as I have argued, necessary to determine the relationship between the three main components of language: the vocabulary, the grammar, and the phonology. Related to the problem of deciding whether language should be regarded as a system is the problem of deciding whether the word, as apparently believed by Saussure, Bühler, and Vygotsky, or the sentence, as believed by Chomsky, Wundt, and many modern grammarians, should be regarded as the linguistic unit, or whether, as I believe, the word and the sentence are two different types of units. To deal adequately with these questions a better understanding of the *functions* of language is needed. In my judgement in order to handle more productively the problems mentioned, scientists must construct models in which attempts are made to relate thinking, behaviour, and language to each other and in which the relationship between the vocabulary, the grammar, and the phonology is specified. When such models have been constructed scientists must find ways of evaluating the models. The construction and evaluation of such models require other procedures than those recommended by positivist thinkers. In the next chapter I shall discuss such procedures.

For the construction of useful, comprehensive scientific models, knowledge of a variety of different types are needed. Most likely much of the material collected by psychologists will prove valuable for future theory construction. However, at present it is difficult to decide which of the facts they have produced affect current conceptions of language. In my opinion the light psychologists have shed on the relationship between perception and language is of particular importance. The social anthropologists Brent Berlin and Paul Kay (1969) showed that the words for colour in a number of languages seem to reflect properties of the visual system and Elionor Rosch (1973) found that the terms the different languages have for the denotation of colour do not affect the capacity for colour discrimination. These results make clear that colour perception is not determined by language. In contrast the results show that the meaning of linguistic signs denoting colour reflects the structure of colour perception. Clark and Clark (ibid) have also argued persuasively that words used for the denotation of shape reflect properties of the perceptual system. Furthermore, Miller and Johnson-Laird (ibid) have argued convincingly that the meaning of many types of words can be seen as reflecting perceptual operations. Evidence that language does not structure perception, but, on the contrary, is itself structured by perception, is thus accumulating.

So far psychologists do not seem to have produced evidence that thinking and language represent different capacities. However, because it is reasonable to believe that thinking is closely dependent upon perception, the finding that perception is not structured by language adds strength to the belief that thinking and language are different things. In Chapter 2 I shall discuss the relationship between thinking and language. At this point I shall just call attention to the fact that a number of attempts have been made to test the Whorfian hypothesis, but so far no attempt has brought results which support it. This may be taken as an indication that it is wrong. (For reviews of research on the Whorfian hypothesis, see Clark and Clark, ibid; Glass and Holyoak, ibid.)

The study of the acquisition of language in the child is hampered by the fact that current conceptions of language are so unclear. Still, the study of language development in the child has produced some important facts about language. Language development seems to begin in the way that the child produces utterances containing one single sign which resembles the words of adult speech. Some research workers have argued that these utterances represent fragmentary, incomplete sentences, so- called holophrases. However, if one does not assume that thinking and language are inseparable, there is in the first place no need to assume that verbal communication must take place by means of grammatical sentences. Secondly, one does not find any trace of grammatical features in these early utterances. Hence, it is reasonable to regard the first utterances of the child as one-word utterances. Lois Bloom (1973) has given a detailed argument for this position. Following the one-word utterance, the child will for a period of time make a number of utterances containing two words which do not seem to be related to each other by grammatical rules. Then again the child begins gradually to use morphemes denoting grammatical relationships. The child's acquisition of grammatical rules seems to take place in the way that the rules are learnt one by one, i.e. in a piecemeal fashion, as was originally found by Roger Brown (1973). Useful reviews of work concerning the relationship between psychology and language have been made by Clark and Clark (ibid); Blumenthal (1970, 1985); John Carroll (1985).

Treatment of problems of language within physiology and biology

Empirical research on the relationship between language and the brain has been carried on since around 1860 when Paul Broca made the epoch making discovery that a lesion to the side of the left frontal lobe resulted in a speech disorder, in aphasia. Shortly after Broca had reported his discovery, Carl Wernicke showed that a lesion in the temporal lobe in the left hemisphere also led to disturbances in linguistic performance. Wernicke also presented a theory about the functions of the areas discovered by Broca and himself, and related the two areas to each other. He assumed that the posterior area, the area discovered by himself, was responsible for the perception and comprehension of speech and that the anterior area, the area discovered by Broca, was responsible for the execution of speech, for the motor aspect. In the 1960s Norman Geschwind revived

Wernicke's theory, pointed out that it could account fairly adequately for the various types of aphasia, and supplemented it with new data and elaborated on it. (For brief histories of the study of aphasia, see Michael Arbid and David Caplan, 1979; Ivar Reinvang, 1985.)

The earlier—and most of the present—studies of aphasia have been based on the performance of patients suffering from strokes or in some other way having received lesions to some part of their brains. On the basis of a lesion to some specific part of the brain it is naturally not possible to draw firm conclusions concerning the function of this part of the brain. Also, as emphasized by Harry Goodglass (1979)—and other experienced research workers on problems of aphasia—the effects of lesions differ from brain to brain, are influenced by age, handedness as well as by individual differences in brain organization. Due to problems, such as those mentioned, it has been difficult to find adequate procedures for testing the hypotheses advanced by Broca, Wernicke and other research workers dealing with problems of brain damage. Though by now the following points seem to be widely accepted.

In right-handed adult individuals adequate linguistic performance requires that the Broca and Wernicke areas and the neural connections between them are intact. However, there is disagreement as to how these areas are more precisely to be circumscribed. In the overwhelming proportions of instances right-handed people have the two areas in their left hemisphere. On the basis of these findings it seems plausible to conclude that the capacity for language is dependent upon specific cortical structures. However, as emphasized by Eric Lenneberg (1967), children who have acquired some language and whose dominant hemisphere has been ablated, do still acquire language. Apparently, when Broca's and Wernicke's areas have been removed, other areas can take over as the child develops. Hence the relationship between the capacity for language and the brain cannot simply be stated in the way that this capacity is dependent upon specific parts of the brain. The conclusion which can be drawn is that the capacity for language is dependent upon a certain organization of the brain, and that in most instances when the brain has been developed, the capacity for language is dependent upon the areas discovered by Broca and Wernicke.

By now it also seems to be widely accepted that lesions to Broca's and Wernicke's areas have different effects on linguistic performance. The following rather cautious conclusions arrived at by Geschwind (1979) would probably be acceptable to most modern aphasiologists:

> A lesion in either Broca's area or Wernicke's area leads to a disruption of speech, but the nature of the two disorders is quite different. In Broca's aphasia speech is labored and slow and articulation is impaired. The response to a question will often make sense, but

> it generally cannot be expressed as a fully formed or grammatical sentence. There is particular difficulty with the inflection of verbs, with pronouns and connective words and with complex grammatical constructions. As a result the speech has a telegraphic style. (...)
> In Wernicke's aphasia speech is phonetically and even grammatically normal, but it is semantically deviant. Words are often strung together with considerable facility and with the proper inflections, so that the utterance has the recognizable structure of a sentence. The words chosen, however, are often inappropriate, and they sometimes include nonsensical syllables or words. Even when the individual words are correct, the utterance as a whole may express its meaning in a remarkably roundabout way.

Some research workers have concluded that Wernicke's area is mainly responsible for the semantical aspect of language, while Broca's area is mainly responsible for articulation and syntax. (For a review of results which support this conclusion, see Glass and Holyoak, ibid.) If this conclusion could be established, it would provide evidence that the semantical component may have evolved relatively independently of the syntactic and grammatical component of language. In other words, it would provide evidence that language has not evolved as a system in a Saussurean or Chomskian sense. However, while it is plausible to believe that Broca's area is mainly responsible for a capacity for grammar, the type of utterances produced by individuals suffering from lesions in this area can probably be accounted for simply in terms of difficulties with the sequencing of speech as a result of impairment of their motor activity. The fact that Broca aphasics are good readers also runs counter to this belief. In connection with the point discussed it should be noted that it is difficult—if not impossible—to draw a clear line of division between a semantical and a grammatical aspect of language.

While it seems fair to say that up to the present the physiological study of language has produced little factual evidence which has a direct bearing on *conceptions* of language, some important evidence has been produced. For a long time it has been known that individuals suffering from some damage to the brain may lose their capacity for language while their capacity for thinking seems to be fairly well retained. This suggests that thinking may occur independently of language. More recently this conclusion has received support from the results of studies of the performance of individuals in which fibers connecting the two hemispheres have been severed. In right-handed individuals it has been shown that they may not be capable of naming an object placed in the right hand or presented visually to the left half of the visual field, while they are capable of identifying the object. (For a review of research on this type of patients, see Glass and Holyoak, ibid.)

As the study of the brain is advanced it is reasonable to believe that neurophysiological evidence may be of central importance in attempts at understanding the nature of language. Yet it must not be overlooked that progress in this type of brain research is highly dependent upon progress in the conceptual analysis of language. Present day neurophysiological research suffers from the weakness that language must be treated as some global entity which includes perception, thinking as well as motivation and emotion. It is naturally difficult to find the neurophysiological correlate for a concept which is so inclusive. As I made clear in my discussion earlier in this chapter, the assistance physiologists can receive from linguistics is highly restricted.

In the 20th century biology has been greatly expanded. Darwin and the early theorists of evolution were not able to reconcile the theory of evolution with knowledge accumulating within genetics. When this reconciliation was brought about in the 1930s, the theory was provided with a much more solid basis. Biology was further expanded by combining it with knowledge from the most advanced empirical sciences, physics and chemistry. The progress in biology naturally resulted in attempts at viewing language in the perspective of biological evolution.

During the last decades zoologists have extensively and intensively studied communication in animals. This work has made clear the great importance communication has for the adjustment of many animals to their environment. The results of this research give added weight to the belief that language has evolved out of earlier forms of communication in the primate species. By combining the results of studies of communication and cognition in primate species with knowledge of the evolution of the brain, scientists, such as Sherwood Washburn and collaborators (Washburn and Shirley Strum, 1972; Washburn and Elisabeth McCown, 1978) and Richard Passingham (1982) have been capable of shedding considerable light on questions concerning the relationship between thinking, communication, and language. In this connection mention should also be made of the fact that comparative work on the anatomy of the sensory systems and comparative work on the perceptual discriminatory capacities of the primates show that sensory perception in the primate species have fundamental characteristics in common. It seems to be a highly plausible assumption that individuals of the non-human primate species perceive the physical world in a manner which is highly similar to that of man. This is strong evidence against the idea of Humboldt—cherished by so many thinkers of the 20th century—that language structures perception. As I mentioned in the section on psychology and language, a rejection of this belief considerably weakens the belief that language structures thinking.

When in the 1950s behaviourist psychologists tried to explain language, they did so on the basis of principles which they claimed had a general validity not only for the mammalian species, but also for other classes of animals. The fact that speech presupposes particular anatomical structures and particular physiological processes was left out of consideration. Research workers, such as Lenneberg (ibid), who viewed language in the perspective of biological evolution, adduced evidence which made clear that to explain how language was acquired through learning, it was essential to take into account the fact that it has a specific biological foundation. Lenneberg pointed out that—in contrast to what was assumed by behaviourists—naming could *not* be explained in terms of associative learning. Naming, he argued, is a very complicated process. A main point in Lenneberg's approach was that the development of language in children had to be understood as a maturational process. Unfortunately in his account of the ontogenetic development of language he did not explain how perceptual and other cognitive factors interact with motor factors. He tended to conceive of use of language as some comprehensive, global entity which could not be analyzed into parts traceable down the phylogenetic scale. The result was that he came to regard the use of language one-sidedly as an activity discontinuous with activities found in the non-human primate species. Apparently, whether one wants to emphasize the continuity or discontinuity in the evolution of language is dependent upon the way one defines 'language'. In my judgement, at the present state of knowledge it is not wise to try to settle the problem of definition. This means that scientists must try to make clear what use of language has in common with activities found in the other non-human primate species as well as what sets use of language apart from other types of activities. Though, even if Lenneberg took an unbalanced view of the problem of continuity versus discontinuity and was unclear on questions concerning maturation, he contributed to a better understanding of the phylo- and ontogenetic development of language. Mention should also be made of the fact that he contributed to a widening of the perspective on the ontogenetic development by bringing into the discussion results from investigations of abnormal language development found in children suffering from handicaps, such as deafness, blindness, and effects of chromosomal aberrations found in children exhibiting Down's syndrome.

One way of investigating the biological foundations of language is to study the effects of specific procedures for teaching non-human primates to use symbols for communication. All through the 20th century animal psychologists have tried to teach apes to use symbols for communication. When it was discovered that apes were lacking an anatomical structure which allowed them to produce words, psychologists devised procedures which allowed them to use other types of symbols than spoken words. Since the end of the 1960s extensive work has been carried out to find out the extent to which apes can use symbols (such as hand signs, three-dimensional plastic pieces, and two-dimensional graphic signs). In the 1970s Allen and Beatrice Gardner (1970), David Premack (1971), and others reported results which seemed to reveal a surprising capacity for use of language in chimpanzees of the species *Pan troglodytes*. However, this research was critized for being based on inadequate conceptions of language and lack of experimental controls. (An anthology of articles critical of the studies performed in the 1970s has been collected and provided with an introduction by Thomas Sebeok and Jean Umiker-Sebeok, 1980.) As pointed out by Washburn (1973), primates can easily learn to associate meanings with visual and auditory inputs, but this fact need not mean that they have a capacity for language. It is, as argued by Herbert Terrace (1985), necessary to show that the apes use symbols with an understanding that the symbols can be used for communication. After having critically examined available evidence Terrace concluded that it is still hardly possible to arrive at a firm conclusion on this point. Elsewhere (Saugstad, 1980) I have argued that to understand that a sign is a name for something one must understand that the sign can be used for communication. Lenneberg was probably right when he held that naming was a far more complicated process than the behaviourists had assumed. I think it must still be regarded as controversial whether chimpanzees are capable of using names for communication. While it naturally is difficult to say what more precisely can be meant by intended actions in the use of symbols, Sue Savage-Rumbaugh et al. (1986, p. 213) may have given a fairly adequate summary of present evidence on the issue concerning the use of symbols for communication with apes:

> The weight of the evidence to date suggests that apes tend to learn symbols in an associational manner, and they need explicit systematic training in order to enable them to use symbols referentially and to respond appropriately and competently as listeners. However, once they are given such training, their symbol usage begins to take on an increasingly representational character until finally they are able to use symbols to convey intended actions.

More recently Savage-Rumbaugh and coworkers (1984, 1985, a and b; 1986) made the surprising discovery that another species of chimpanzee (*Pan paniscus*) than the species ordinarily seen in the zoo (*Pan troglodytes*) seems to be able spontaneously (i.e. without specific training) to use symbols for communication, and what is even more surprising seems to be able to comprehend the meaning of a number of words from hearing these words in the speech of its caretakers. A characteristic of man's capacity for using language is that children seem spontaneously to use words for communication. If individuals of the species *Pan paniscus* spontaneously use symbols for communication they meet an important requirement for being ascribed a capacity for use of language. However, it should be noted that in order to be ascribed a spontaneous use of symbols for communication it must be shown that without specific training by human individuals they spontaneously use symbols in communication with fellow individuals. Also, if they are capable of—as they seem to be—understanding fragments of speech without being specifically trained, they meet another important requirement for being ascribed a capacity for using language.

So far the results of attempts to teach use of symbols for communication to apes indicate that even with intensive training apes will acquire a limited number of symbols for communicatory use. Furthermore, their use of grammatical rules is at best highly rudimentary. Still further, their capacity for producing signs either vocally or manually is most likely extremely limited. Yet the results of this research are important because they help us understand how the evolution of language may have been a continuous process. As I shall argue in Chapter 3, the step from using a limited number to that of using a larger number of symbols for communication may not be so great. Further, if it can be shown—as I think it can—that grammar has a basis in perception and thinking, it may not be so difficult to understand the development from the use of a combination of signs, as found in apes, to that of combining signs by means of grammatical rules.

As made clear by Savage-Rumbaugh et al. (1985, a, p. 180), the efforts to teach language to apes have contributed to deepening and widening the scientists' conceptions of language:

> In our efforts to teach language to *Pan troglodytes*, we have found that we have learned as much, if not more, from our failures as from our successes. The chimpanzees' halting acquisition of symbols has taught us that language is not made of whole cloth, but of many pieces. It is not merely symbols, or combinations of symbols, but complex ways of interacting, and complex sorts of inter-individual expectancies that intertwine and coordinate behaviour. Symbols are the medium of language, but not its substance. Its substance is planned, coordinated cooperation achieved only through mutual telling and mutual expectancies regarding that telling. These expectancies must be shaped by common past experiences and such experiences must occur in an atmosphere of trust and cooperation. Language, in short, is a part of culture; it is living, breathing, ever-changing, behavioural culture. It does not leave tangible artefacts, but it changes the behaviour of groups in a drastic manner. It cannot belong to one person; it is the property of inter-individual interactions. Without such interactions, language, as we know it, does not exist.

The biologically oriented psychologists' attempts at shedding light on the nature of language have led them far away from the formal conceptions of language providing the foundations of linguistics. In contrast to linguists they stress that language is not made of whole cloth, but of many pieces and—in agreement with the findings of cultural anthropologists—that its use represents complex ways of interacting, that it is planned, coordinated behaviour, and that it must take place in an atmosphere of cooperation. However, strange as it may sound, the behaviouristically oriented psychologists fail to underline that use of language presupposes a skill in communication, what Hymes termed 'communicatory competence'.

To communicate effectively by means of symbols, as I shall argue in Chapter 7, an individual must be capable of understanding what kind of knowledge is available to fellow individuals and must further be capable of transmitting to fellow individuals knowledge which can supplement their available knowledge. This transmittance of information is, as I have argued elesewhere (Saugstad, 1980), a skill in which the capacities for producing and comprehending speech interact in complex and subtle ways.

Before I leave the discussion of the discovery made by Savage-Rumbaugh and collaborators I shall just point out that one straightforward interpretation of their finding that an individual of the species *Pan paniscus* was capable of comprehending speech, is that prior to being exposed to speech this individual had developed a capacity for perceiving and thinking which allowed him to assign meaning to various linguistic signs. According to this way of looking at matters, the finding suggests that a thinking which makes possible a rudimentary understanding of language may develop independently of use of language. In other words, it indicates that thinking and language are two different things.

The expansion which has taken place in biological knowledge during the last decades has also resulted in a revival of interest in the problem of the origin of language and in the 1970s this problem was discussed in two large symposia (J.-H. Scharf, 1975; Stevan Harnad, Horst Steklis, and Jane Lancaster, 1976). While speculations about the origin of language help to give perspective on linguistic research, it should be noted that even if at present we lack factual knowledge about the evolution of language in the hominid species, it is possible on the basis of the general evolution of the primate species to make highly plausible inferences as to the relationship between perception and thinking on the one hand, and language on the other hand.

Before I finish these remarks on the biological foundations of language I want to say a few words on the hypothesis advanced by Chomsky (1968) that the capacity for forming grammatical sentences is innate. I think it is difficult to formulate this hypothesis so that it can be investigated empirically. Obviously, children acquire language after being exposed to it and—what seems to be overlooked by Chomsky and followers—only after having *practiced* verbal communication for a number of years. Usually children do not seem to master the grammar of their languages until they are 5—6 years old. A great amount of stimulation and practice of various sorts is clearly involved. Until it has been made clear how children learn to communicate verbally, it is hardly possible to say what can be meant by the statement that the capacity for forming sentences is genetically determined. As I have pointed out, the learning involved in speaking correctly grammatically is not simply a question of making inferences from utterances produced by others. It is also a question of obtaining a skill in transmitting information. Also, as I shall argue in Chapter 7, the fact that people tend to speak in grammatical sentences reflects the structure of man's perception and thinking, and it is not possible to make clear what is meant by a 'grammatical sentence' unless this structure is taken into account. The grammarian's formal definition of a sentence is inadequate for empirical research which aims at demonstrating that the capacity for forming sentences is genetically determined. Of course, I am not arguing against the belief that in some way this capacity may be genetically determined. The point I am making is that Chomsky and his followers have not been able to formulate the problem in such a way that it can be given an empirical interpretation.

Conclusion

This brief and summary review of linguistic research shows that all the disciplines considered have given important contributions to our understanding of language. The review also shows that in order to arrive at an adequate conception of language it is necessary to take not only the perspective of the linguists, but also the perspectives of cultural anthropologists, psychologists, physiologists, and zoologists. Research workers within all of these disciplines have called attention to important aspects and facts about language. Cultural anthropologists have emphasized the fact that language originates in the speech community and that it is a means of interaction between individuals in a culture. Psychologists of a behaviourist persuasion have emphasized the fact that use of language is behaviour. Psychologists have also shed light on the relationship language has to perception and thinking, and child psychologists have established the important facts about language that in the acquisition of it children begin by producing one-word utterances, then two-word utterances, and then finally successively include grammatical features in their speech. Physiologists have documented that right-handed individuals have specific areas necessary for speech, and further that lesions respectively to Broca's and Wernicke's areas lead to different types of deficiencies in language performance. Lesions to the former area result in difficulties in articulation and the sequencing of speech whereas lesions to the latter area result in difficulties in understanding words and in using them in an appropriate manner. Zoologists have called attention to the fact that language has evolved in man's phylogenesis and have together with animal psychologists produced knowledge which allows scientists to discern lines in this evolution. Previously in this chapter I discussed a number of facts about language which have been produced by linguists. To develop an approach which will make research more productive, scientists must find ways of combining these facts about language with the facts produced by cultural anthropologists, psychologists, physiologists, and zoologists into a unitary conception of language.

Chapter 2

Language is an expression of thoughts

Our understanding of the world is achieved more effectively by conceptual improvements than by the discovery of new facts, even though the two are not mutually exclusive.

Ernst Mayr. *The Growth of Biological Thought*. 1981. p. 23.

In Chapter 1 I pointed out that in an attempt at delimiting language as a field of research one meets with the problem of deciding whether the capacities for thinking and using language should be regarded as separable or inseparable. In that chapter I also called attention to the fact that in order to relate psychology to language one must decide whether or not thinking and language are separable. Still further, I mentioned that in the Saussurean conception of language as a system the meaning of words was determined by their relationships to each other and not by reference to extra-linguistic facts. Hence, also for a discussion of meaning it is of central importance to clarify the relationship between thinking and language. Of course, when one believes that language is an expression of thoughts one also believes that thinking represents an activity distinguishable from that of using language. Apparently one also assumes that use of language has a basis in thinking. In the present chapter I shall discuss the relationship between thinking and language.

Before one proceeds to this discussion I think it is wise to bring to mind that for at least 200 years thinkers have disagreed as to how they should conceive of the relationship between thinking and language. This suggests that there can be no simple solution to the problem of relating thinking to language. Also, it should be borne in mind that at the present state of knowledge the scientists' ideas about thinking and language are so vague and diffuse that it is frequently difficult to decide what is to count as evidence for the one or the other position.

The belief that language is an expression of thoughts does probably originate in reflections of the following type. There seems to be a close relationship between, on the one hand, cognitive activities, such as perceiving, remembering, imagining, and thinking, and, on the other hand, use of language. Furthermore, the cognitive activities mentioned seem to take place irrespectively of whether or not speaking is going on.

On the basis of these two types of reflections it is assumed that somehow language is a representation of thoughts (entities produced by the cognitive activities mentioned). I think it must be admitted that this way of conceiving of language is a natural one.

The belief that language is an expression of thoughts has been supported by a number of philosophers and empirical psychologists. In addition to René Descartes mention should here be made of John Locke and the British empiricist philosophers and in more recent times of phenomenologically oriented philosophers, such as Franz Brentano and Edmund Husserl. In the beginning of the 20th century and up to the Second World War most European psychologists—of the East as well as of the West—seem to have taken more or less for granted that somehow language is an expression of thoughts. In more recent times Jean Piaget is a well known defender of the belief, and during the last decades the widely accepted information processing approach to the study of psychology seems to be based on assumptions which are in agreement with it.

The opposite view on the relationship between thinking and language probably arises out of considerations of the following type. Frequently thinking seems to be carried out as an internal dialogue, a dialogue in which the thinker communicates with an imaginary listener. Further, when one thinks of some topic it seems to present itself in terms of verbal expressions and frequently the thoughts seem to be accompanied by words. Moreover, in many—possibly most—instances speaking seems to go on without any awareness of the fact that thoughts of various sorts are expressed. As I mentioned in Chapter 1, the idea that thinking and language are inseparable was for the first time forcibly presented by Herder in the latter half of the 18th century and was elaborated by Humboldt in the first half of the 19th century. In the 20th century it appeared in approaches taken to the study of language by Saussure, Sapir, Whorf and a number of other research workers. Of course, there is a difference between the belief that thinking and language are inseparable and the belief that language structures thinking. I shall first consider the former belief and then at the end of the chapter discuss the problem of how language affects thinking.

It should be noted that the belief that thinking and language are inseparable became central in analytic philosophy, which came to dominate British, American, and Scandinavian philosophy. Hence, linguists who searched for a foundation for their treatment of problems in analytic philosophy of language got the Herder-Humboldt idea in a double dose. In a letter to the British philosopher Benno Kerry Gottlob Frege (1892, p. 45)—who was a great stimulator to the linguistic philosophers of the 20th century—emphasized that in dealing with problems of logic the point of departure was most naturally taken in considerations as to how language is used:

> Kerry holds that no logical rules can be based on linguistic distinctions; but my own way of doing this is something that nobody can avoid who lays down such rules at all; for we cannot come to an understanding with one another apart from language, and so in the end we must always rely on other people's understanding words, inflexions, and sentence-construction in essentially the same way as ourselves.

Quine (1960, p. 3) stated his belief concerning the relationship between thinking and language in the following manner: "Conceptualization on any considerable scale is inseparable from language, and our ordinary language of physical things is about as basic as language gets". As I have already mentioned, Quine was an adherent of the stimulus-response paradigm and thought he might give a useful account of language and meaning by applying this paradigm. Ludwig Wittgenstein (1953, sec. 32) expressed his belief concerning the relationship between thinking and language in a commentary to Augustine's account of how language is acquired by the child. This commentary once greatly affected my own view of language acquisition and certainly has affected that of many other empirical research workers, and I shall quote it:

> And now, I think, we can say: Augustine describes the learning of human language as if the child came into a strange country and did not understand the language of the country; that is, as if it already had a language, only not this one.

In a book on Frege, Michael Dummett (1981, pp. 39—40) has recently summed up the position of analytic philosophers:

> The basic tenet of analytical philosophy, common to such disparate philosophers as Schlick, early and late Wittgenstein, Carnap, Ryle, Ayer, Austin, Quine and Davidson, may be expressed as being that the philosophy of thought is to be aquated with the philosophy of language: more exactly, (i) an account of language does not presuppose an account of thought, (ii) an account of language yields an account of thought, and (iii) there is no other adequate means by which an account of thought may be given.

Apparently, considerations based upon introspective evidence cannot settle the disagreement between the two camps. Nor can it be settled by a logical examination of language. Evidence of a different nature must be found. As I made clear in Chapter 1, the study of aphasia as well as studies of the performance of split-brain patients indicate that thinking and language are different things and so does a study of the performance of children prior to the onset of speech. However, studies of these types allow of different interpretations. More decisive evidence on the issue is found in the study of the evolution of the primate species and I shall concentrate on this study.

Thinking and language in the perspective of biological evolution

The work which has produced knowledge about the evolution of the primate species has been undertaken within a number of different disciplines: paleontology, comparative anatomy, molecular biology, physiology, archaeology, and animal psychology. The study of the evolution of the primates illustrates how science is the art of weaving together weak strains of evidence into a solid fabric. One type of evidence considered in isolation may seem meagre indeed. However, when it is combined with evidence from other sources definite points in evolution may be established as highly plausible. I am mentioning this because research workers unfamiliar with the study of the primate evolution may easily come to suspect that the knowledge available has no firm basis. There are many lacunae in this work. Particularly there are important gaps in our knowledge of the evolution of the hominids and the circumstances under which use of language evolved. However, in a rough sort of way it is possible to present a plausible picture of the evolution of the perceptual and intellective capacities of the primates. For my argument I do not think knowledge of the more exact development of the capacity for language in the hominids is needed. What is needed is knowledge of communication and cognitive processes in individuals of the non-human primate species.

I shall focus my argument on the fact that man and the great apes have a common ancestor. This is useful because we can have a high degree of certainty that the individuals who were the common ancestors of the *Hominidae* and *Pongidae* had not yet acquired a system of symbols for communication. If they had acquired such a system, this must have been lost in the further evolution of the great apes and it is implausible that so highly adaptive a capacity should have disappeared. On the basis of a general knowledge of the evolution of the primates it seems reasonable to conclude that the individuals who were the common ancestors of man, and the great apes, had capacities for communication and cognition more or less similar to those we find in apes today. Furthermore, it is reasonable to believe that the capacity for cognition has evolved relatively independently of the capacity for communication and consequently that the two capacities should be distinguished. Also, the fact that intellective capacities were so well developed prior to the acquisition of language *strongly suggests that use of language must have a basis in cognition.* My argument has the following two main premises: 1. The common ancestors of the Hominidae and Pongidae did not possess a system of symbols which they used for communication and 2. they possessed a highly developed capacity for understanding and thinking.

1. Individuals of the non-human primates have a variety of means of communication. They communicate by postures, facial expressions, movements of eyes and limbs and body, and vocalisations. (For a review of primate communication, see Peter Marler, 1977.) However, apart from the fact that they possibly may be able to communicate that specific types of enemies are approaching, they do not seem to have a system of symbols which allows them to communicate about the external world. Communication in these species seems mainly to be an expression of emotional states. Washburn and Strum (1972, p. 479) have summed up what they believed to be the main points concerning communication in individuals of the non-human primate species:

> Communication in the nonhuman primates may be considered as functioning primarily to convey the emotional states of the actors in the social system. Sounds form only a small part of the communication system, and the sounds have minimal meanings apart from the patterned sequences of social behaviors. It is only by viewing communication as a social adaptation that an adequate model for understanding nonhuman sound communication can be developed.

2. It is known that monkeys and apes have perceptual capacities very similar to those found in *Homo sapiens*. Furthermore, as is evident from observations as well as experiments, they are great problem solvers. Even if their capacity for anticipating future events probably is considerably lower than that found in man, they possess this capacity. From observation and experiment we know that they learn from watching each other. Also, they may possibly be credited with a capacity for following rules. (For a review of cognitive capacities in the non-human primates, see Richard Passingham, 1982.) In other words, monkeys and apes are capable of reacting to a great variety of relationships and to draw a number of different types of inferences. Their behaviour indicates that they are capable of performing tasks which involve capacities closely resembling those which are designated as thinking in human individuals.

Against my assertion that the common ancestors of man and the great apes possessed highly developed cognitive capacities one might object that the common ancestors might have belonged to a species ranking low on the primate scale. This is unlikely. Present evidence makes it plausible to believe that the common ancestors ranked high on the scale.

Our great biological similarity to the chimpanzee suggests a very close relationship to this species and the common ancestors might have belonged to a species which in intellectual capacity did not rank far below it. Even if the common ancestors should have ranked rather low on the primate scale, they did probably possess well developed cognitive capacities.

It will be noted that the question to what extent it is possible to teach monkeys and apes to use symbols for communicatory purposes is not relevant to the problem I have discussed. The question I have raised is whether or not highly developed cognitive capacities have evolved independently of communication and language. In order to answer this question we must obtain knowledge on how induviduals of non-human primate species behave in the wild and not what they can be instructed to do.

Because the capacity for thinking evolved prior to the capacity for symbolic communication, it is reasonable to assume that language has a basis in thinking. However, even if one accepts that language has this basis, one might still hold that language governed man's thinking and hence, that thinking and language are not separable. This argument seems to be valid only if we restrict the use of the term 'thinking' to refer to thinking of the most abstract and highly developed kind. In dealing with problems of thinking one may easily come to overlook performances in tasks which seem closely related to perceptual tasks, but which involve complicated organizations of different types of experiences. A study of the evolution primates have undergone—and which our ancestors underwent in their arboreal existence—may help counteract the tendency to overlook that a number of highly automatized performances can be most reasonably regarded as involving thought processes. In primates adapted to a life in the trees the forefeet were changed into hands, and the fingertips obtained a great sensitivity, foveal and stereoscopic vision developed. But, also —and now I am approaching types of performances involving thought processes—fine coordinations between vision and movements of fingers, hands, arms and legs evolved. This coordination is learnt and involves the organization of dissimilar types of experiences. To be able to move as skillfully in the trees as the primates do, an organism must be in the possession of a capacity for making a variety of complicated judgements. For example, the strength of branches visually perceived must be evaluated. To land safely on a branch estimates must be made of the time required from the moment one branch is left and another branch is reached. To avoid predators, primates must learn to judge how fast *they* can run or climb a certain distance and how fast their predators can run or climb the same distance.

Performances, such as those mentioned, which concern coordination between visual impressions and movements of hands and limbs, judgement of distances, orientation to physical objects, judgement of velocities in moving objects, effects of pressures upon physical bodies, etc. involve complex learning and should not be considered as perceptual. They are clearly not to reflexes, and even if they may have an instinctual basis they are not to be regarded to as instincts. They are complicated cognitive processes on the borderline between perception and abstract thinking. It is hardly possible to understand the nature of thinking unless performances of these types are taken into account. They are probably involved in all types of thinking. It will be understood that it would not be an advantage to an organism that performances such as those mentioned were governed by language. On the contrary, it would be a a great disadvantage. *The idea that language once acquired began to govern the thought processes which had evolved prior to the acquisition of language is not plausible.*

In view of the present evidence it seems highly plausible to believe that in phylogenesis understanding and thinking have evolved independently of language and that use of language has a basis in understanding and thinking. Furthermore, it is plausible to believe that the relationship between understanding and thinking on the one hand, and language on the other, is preserved through the ontogenetic development. According to this way of looking at matters, the belief that thinking and language are inseparable must be rejected.

The conclusion I have arrived at is hardly a surprise to thinkers in the European phenomenonological tradition of philosophy and psychology, nor to developmental psychologists in the Piagetian tradition, nor to modern research workers of cognition in the information processing tradition. However, it runs counter to the Herder-Humboldtian tradition and thus to central beliefs in Saussure, members of the Prague School of linguistics and to beliefs advanced by Whorf and Sapir. Also, it is in opposition to the belief of analytic and linguistic philosophy which, as expressed by Dummett, is that "an account of language does not presuppose an account of thought, that an account of language yields an account of thought, and that there is no other adequate means by which an account of thought may be given". On the basis of the conclusion I have arrived at it seems natural to believe that *if scientists are to understand the nature of language they must begin by trying to understand the nature of thinking.*

If language has a basis in thinking it is natural to believe that an understanding of the meaning of words must be achieved by a consideration of the structure which perception and thinking have. Instead of searching for the meaning of words in a study of the relationships between the words of a language, it is natural to search for their meaning in extra-linguistic facts. The conclusion arrived at throws doubt on the Saussurean belief that language can fruitfully be conceived of as a system. Also it hould be realized that the conclusion has a bearing on the Chomskian conception of language as a system of internalized rules. In the first place, it will be understood that the fact emphasized by Humboldt and Chomsky that in use of language speakers make infinite use of finite resources, may not be a fact about language, but simply a fact about man's capacity for thinking. Secondly, it will be understood that in order to account for use of language by means of a set of rules, it is essential that the relationship between these rules and thinking should be clarified. This is essential, because a defining characteristic of thinking seems to be that it is not merely a following of a set of rules. It does not take much reflection to understand that a clarification of this relationship represents an extremely complicated task. However, until this task has been handled it is difficult to see what is involved in the assertion that language is a set of internalized rules.

Terminological discussion

Behaviourists believed that they might infer cognitive processes from behaviour and many of them also thought that they might account for these processes in terms of the stimulus- response paradigm. By now it seems fairly clear that the terminology suggested by the behaviourists did not allow of a more precise description than the introspective psychology to which the behaviourists reacted. For example, the accounts given of language and meaning relatively recently by Skinner and Quine are based upon a loose and vague use of the term 'stimulus'. Elsewhere (Saugstad, 1977) I have discussed difficulties met with by behaviourists in attempts at describing mammalian behaviour. When the behaviourist claim is discarded *the only alternative left for scientists wanting to study the behaviour involved in use of language seems to be to describe as accurately as possible this behaviour by means of words which in everyday language designates cognitive processes.* In line with this conclusion I shall adopt a number of words from everyday language which I shall try to clarify by a consideration of what I believe to be some important knowledge about cognition.

Not only the Indo-European languages, but probably all languages of the world have a number of words for describing cognitive processes. The very fact that these words are understood indicates that speakers have considerable knowledge about cognitive processes. Barwise and Perry (1983, p. 229) have drawn attention to the remarkable ability human individuals have for understanding perception, thought, and action:

> Common-sense folk psychology contains a good deal of knowledge about human perception, thought, and action. Indeed, when one

> considers the complexity of the nervous system, our ability to understand perception, thought, and action in the way that is necessary for the most commonplace human interactions is surely mankind's most extraordinary intellectual accomplishment to date, and is a precondition of most other such accomplishments, since it is a precondition of language.

When account is taken of the ability human individuals have for understanding cognitive processes, it will be realized that careful descriptions of the behaviour involved in use of language may have a rather solid basis, even if it is undertaken in terms of words of everyday language.

Psychologists have traditionally divided the study of cognition into the parts: perception, memory, imagination, and thinking. Yet it must be realized that these parts are closely dependent upon each other and not easily distinguishable. It is hardly possible to conceive of a capacity for thinking without at the same time conceiving of a capacity for perceiving and for capacities for remembering and imagining. We draw a line of distinction between tasks in which an individual must react to a stimulation which is present at the point in time at which the reaction occurs, and tasks in which objects are handled which are not directly perceived. This distinction is important, but it does not take much reflection to understand that it is difficult to decide what can be meant by direct perception. What an individual perceives is dependent upon not only the physical stimulation, but also upon organismic factors, such as attention or set. Apparently the organism has a capacity for directing its attention and for selecting information from the physical stimulation. Should this capacity be regarded as a capacity for thinking or does it form part of perception? The difficulty in answering this question suggests that it is not possible to distinguish clearly between perception and thinking. On the one hand, thinking seems to be closely dependent upon perception and, on the other hand, the capacity for thinking in individuals of the primate species represents an important aspect of the evolution of these species. There is no simple solution to the problem of distinguishing between thinking and perception.

Another difficulty in handling the term 'thinking' arises from the fact that the word "thinking" is frequently used when a conscious effort of some sort is involved; the thinker is confronted with some task or problem which is not immediately solved. However, in many tasks of an intellectual nature we may not be aware of any effort, not aware of the fact that we are confronted with a particular problem. For example, we add figures without being aware of any efforts, take right and left turns in streets to arrive at certain places without being aware of the fact that we thereby are solving problems. The types of performances mentioned are not readily designated as thinking. On the other hand, we know that at some stage in the ontogenetic development these types of performances have involved thinking. As a result of having been frequently repeated, the reactions have been automatized. In a treatment of the relationship between thinking and language it would be unsatisfactory to exclude performances which have become automatized. One way of avoiding the difficulty is to use the term 'intelligence' instead of 'thinking'. The former term may be taken to refer to the adaptation of the organism as a whole to the environment. (On this use of the term 'intelligence', see Robert Sternberg, 1982.)

When account is taken of the fact that a large variety of different types of reactions in individuals of the primate species are highly automatized, it is difficult to decide whether they should be conceived of as representing thinking or merely perception or memory. One way of handling this problem is to assume that thinking is involved when different types of experiences have been organized as a result of complicated types of learning. This way of reasoning may frequently be useful in deciding whether or not thinking should be assumed to be involved. But, as the reader will understand, it raises the problem of distinguishing between learning and thinking. By sacrificing this distinction we may come to lose sight of the fact that a fundamental characteristic of cognition in individuals of the primate species is that they are capable of handling novel situations.

As the reader will understand, at the present stage of knowledge it is not possible to arrive at a precise terminology for handling problems in cognition. Adherents of the information processing approach try to account for cognitive tasks by specifying the information or knowledge available to the organism and the operations performed by the organism upon this knowledge. As I have already mentioned, this approach raises the difficulty of determining the nature of the operations and this may lead research workers back to the problem of specifying terms, such as perception, memory, imagination, and thinking. Clearly, the use of the term 'information' or 'knowledge' is not at all unproblematic.

Earlier in the present chapter I have pointed out that it seems difficult to define thinking in such a manner that this capacity is exclusively attributed to human individuals. It is natural to view thinking as a type of processes which relates motor responses to perception. When this position is adopted it is understood that it is hardly possible to find a point in man's phylogenesis at which one can say that thinking originates. In an attempt at tracing down the phylogenetic scale, the capacity for thinking raises the problem of distinguishing between thinking and the basic metabolic processes going on in uni-cellular organisms. A similar difficulty is met with in the study of perception. Also, the reader should note that there is no point on the phylogenetic scale at which we can say that individuals of a species possess concepts. A certain arbitrariness is involved in defining the terms 'perception', 'thinking', 'concept', 'communication' as well as a number of other cognitive terms.

In the discussion of the evolution of thinking and language in the primate species I called attention to the important development which these species underwent as a result of an adaptation to life in the trees. The adaptation which took place was the result of an adaptation to the physical environment. This point is important, because in a study of the use of language and the higher forms of human thinking it is natural to emphasize the social nature of the activities involved, and this may lead one to overlook that the development of thinking cannot be understood merely as a result of social interaction. In the influential account given by George Mead (1934) of the evolution of consciousness he seems to have overlooked this important point. Mead combined certain ideas from Darwin and Wundt. Darwin had suggested that in the course of evolution parts of certain acts involving social relationships might evolve into gestures which would communicate to fellow individuals a particular emotional state. Wundt (1912) elaborated upon this idea and suggested that gestures of the type discussed by Darwin might acquire definite meanings for the individual making the gestures. Like many of his behaviourist contemporaries—Mead believed that he might account for the development of language and the self without making assumptions about emotional states or of consciousness, as done by Darwin and Wundt. He suggested that as a result of interactions between individuals of a certain species, specific acts might be modified in such a way that gestures of various types evolved to which individuals of the species reacted as if they had been complete acts. At some point in the further evolution the individual producing the gestures became capable of reacting to them in the same manner as fellow individuals reacted to it. Still further, these gestures evolved into language. In this manner Mead believed it was possible to explain the development of thinking, the self, and language. As I have already mentioned, one misses in Mead's explanation an account of how the developing individuals become capable of reacting to their own gestures in the same manner as their fellow individuals. While Mead overlooked that an account of the development of communication and language must contain assumptions about a capacity for thinking, he called attention to an important point when he stressed that in order to participate in verbal communication individuals must be capable of taking the attitude, the role, of the individuals with whom they communicate. Also, Mead made an important point in stressing the role communication most likely plays in the development of thinking.

How does language affect thinking?

I have concluded that thinking and use of language are different activities and that language has a basis in thinking. This position does not exclude the possibility that language also affects thinking. There can be no doubt that the use of language greatly affects an individual's knowledge. An individual having acquired language can be instructed by other individuals. This instruction does probably greatly speed up the cognitive development during childhood. Individuals capable of taking part in verbal discourse can share the experiences of other individuals. Through language cultural knowledge of various types is transmitted from one generation to the next and individuals familiar with language have access to this knowledge. So, it is easy to understand that language affects the knowledge of an individual as well as her/his outlook on life. An increase in knowledge does probably give an individual an increased capacity for thinking and in this sense it is not difficult to imagine that language affects thinking. There is also another sense in which it is easy to understand that language may affect the capacity for thinking. As I shall make clear in Chapter 7, to acquire a language is to acquire a skill in communication. In order to learn this skill an individual must learn to solve a variety of different problems. It is reasonable to expect that this increase in problem solving ability makes the individual a better thinker and hence that the acquisition of this skill affects the capacity for thinking. In this connection attention should be drawn to the account given by Vygotsky (1962, 1981) of how language affects thinking. Apparently Vygotsky assumed that prior to acquiring language the child was in the possession of a capacity for thinking. According to him—but not according to all of his students—use of language had a basis in thinking. (For a review of the development of Vygotsky's ideas in Soviet Psychology, see Karl Levitin, 1982.) According to Vygotsky the linguistic sign functions as a tool and by using this tool the intellectual capacity of the child is developed. This gives, I think, a plausible account of how language may affect thinking. Vygotsky's account helps one also to understand how the child's thinking becomes influenced by culture. Language reflects the culture of the speech community of which the child is a part and by interiorizing language by using it, the child is affected by the culture of the speech community.

In our present state of ignorance it is difficult to understand what is going on when an individual is thinking. In some way or other, words may help to structure man's thoughts and thinking might be assumed to be carried on in terms of words. If we assume that thinking can go on without language, thinking carried on by means of words would represent a form of thinking in addition to the one acquired prior to it. Hence, it would probably give a simpler account of thinking to assume that language has a more indirect effect upon thinking. Accordingly, the most appropriate strategy for studying the relationship between thinking and language seems to be to try to explain possible effects of language either as a result of an increase in knowledge, or in terms of an increase in problem solving ability in line with the view I sketched above. However, I want to stress that I do not find it implausible to believe, as done by Allan Paivio and Jan Begg (1981), that during man's ontogeny two symbolic systems are built up which, even if they may interact, also may function as alternative coding systems.

Conclusion

In Chapter 1 mention was made of the fact that the performance of some individuals suffering from aphasia as well as that of children prior to the onset of speech suggests that thinking is not dependent upon language. This suggestion is strongly supported by knowledge about the evolution of the primate species. Furthermore, a study of the evolution of the primates points in the direction that language has a basis in thinking. Hence, available evidence strongly suggests that the Herder-Humboldt hypothesis—on which most of the work of 20th century linguistics and analytic philosophy is based—should be rejected. Instead of conceiving of thinking and language as being inseparable, scientists should begin searching for a basis for language in thinking and perception. Actually, inspiring attempts have more recently been made by Barwise and Perry (1983) to reorient the logicians' study of semantical problems. They have shown that a number of semantical problems can be handled by assuming that linguistic expressions derive their meaning from reference to extralinguistic fact. Of course, I am in agreement with this orientation, as I was in my previous work on language (Saugstad, 1980). The approaches taken by Barwise and Perry and by myself supplement each other. The criticism I raised in Chapter 1 concerns their use of the term 'external situation'. To be able to specify this term in a fruitful manner a basis must be sought *not* in logic and language, but in the scientific study of cognition. The conclusion I have arrived at concerning the relationship between thinking and language seems to be in agreement also with the position John Macnamara (1982) has adopted to the study of the development of language in children.

Chapter 3

Use of language is behaviour

Thought and language have different genetic roots.

Lev S. Vygotsky, *Thought and Language*, p. 41.

Language is a means of communication. That is hardly a matter of dispute. It is easy to point to a variety of different situations in which verbal utterances serve as means of transmitting information from one individual to other individuals. However, while it must be regarded as a well established belief that language is a means of communication, it would give an all too simplified picture of language to say that communication is the only function of language.

Opposing what he assumed to represent the philologists' view of language the cultural anthropologist Bronislaw Malinowski (1923) stressed that language was not the expression of reflected thought. He also argued that language was frequently used to create ties of union between individuals and to maintain stability within groups of individuals. He termed this use 'phatic communion'. I shall give a quote from Malinowski's (1972, pp. 313—314) account of this use of language:

> A mere phrase of politeness, in use as much among savage tribes as in a European drawing-room, fulfils a function to which the meaning of its words is almost completely irrelevant. Inquiries about health, comments on weather, affirmations of some supremely obvious state of things—all such are exchanged, not in order to inform, not in this case to connect people in action, certainly not in order to express any thought. It would be even incorrect, I think, so say that such words serve the purpose of establishing a common sentiment, for this is usually absent from such current phrases of intercourse; and where it purports to exist, as in expressions of sympathy, it is avowedly spurious on one side. What is the r*aison d'etre*, therefore, of such phrases as 'How do you do?' 'Ah, here you are', 'Where do you come from?' 'Nice day to-day'—all of which serve in one society or another as formulae of greeting or approach?

There can be no doubt that Malinowski pointed to a function of language which it would be strained to characterize as communicatory. Phatic communion represents a problem in attempts at accounting for language as a means of transmitting information.

A few years after Malinowski had presented his view of the nature of language, Jean Piaget (1926) drew attention to the fact that language had many functions and that it would be futile to try to reduce them all to that of communicating thought. Probably inspired by Piaget, Ludwig Wittgenstein (1953) used the idea that language has many functions to attack the assumption of Frege and Russell that language has a logical basis. In addition to being used to report, describe, and assert, language is used, he showed, for many other purposes, for example, for asking questions, giving orders, telling stories, thanking, cursing, greeting, and praying. It is hardly possible to account for these uses simply by saying that they are attempts at transmitting information. Inspired by Wittgenstein, but approaching linguistic problems from a somewhat different angle, John Austin (1961, 1962) called attention to the fact that certain utterances could not be construed only as containing a report. They seem, he argued, to involve also a performance relative to the report. For example, one might utter the sentence, "The door is open", with the intention that someone should shut it. This example—as well as numerous others given by Austin and his students—show that it is frequently not unproblematic to say that information is transmitted by means of verbal utterances.

Evidently, a belief to the effect that communication is the only function of language is untenable. Also, Piaget was probably right in holding that it is futile to try to reduce all uses of language to that of communicating thought. However, there is one way of conceiving of the functions of language which, I think is highly plausible and which, when elaborated, may shed important light on the nature of language. Viewing language in the perspective of biological evolution, one may conceive of communication as the original function in the evolution of language and of the other functions as derived from that function. In this sense one may hold that communication is the primary function of language. Below I shall show that the belief that language has originated in communication is in agreement with present knowledge of the evolution of the primates and that alternatives to this belief meet with difficulties. Then I shall show that it is possible to regard uses of language whose functions do not seem to be that of communication, as derived from that function.

Before I turn to these problems I shall comment on Malinowski's point that language is not the expression of reflected thought. Of course, language is sometimes the expression of reflected thought. However, in many instances speaking seems to go on without reflected thought. In the previous chapter I mentioned that in tasks involving much practice, thinking becomes automatized. Speaking and listening are activities which are much practiced. Therefore, it is to be expected that many of the thought processes involved may have become automatized and are not easily registered. For this reason the fact that language is not always an expression of *reflected* thought need not mean that it is not an expression of thought.

The roots of language

In my search for the origin of language I shall concentrate on its roots in communication, thinking, and emotion.

In Chapter 1 I mentioned that during the last decades zoologists have shown that communication plays a great role in the adaptation of a number of different animal species. I emphasized that the primate species have a variety of forms of communication and that these forms are of great importance in their adjustment. Communication serves as a means of keeping groups together and of maintaining a stable social order in the groups. Hence, as emphasized by Washburn and Strum (who were quoted on page 47), communication in individuals of the primate species is closely associated with the social organization of the group. The social nature of communication in the non-human primate species was put to a point by Steven Green and Peter Marler (1979, p. 75) when they wrote: "A communicatory interaction is a social event. It is the essence of sociability". In human societies language plays a central role in the interactions taking place between the individuals and in regulating their social relationships. It is, therefore, natural to assume—as most biologists seem to do—that language has evolved out of the more primitive forms of communication found in the non-human primate species. In other words, it is natural to believe that language has originated as a means of communication. By adopting this belief one can understand the social nature of language. Present knowledge of the evolution of man is all too fragmentary to allow scientists to construct theories of the evolution of language which are firmly based on empirical evidence. Though, when account is taken of the fact that language has one root in communication and one in perception and thinking, it seems possible to understand how language has evolved out of the more primitive forms of communication found in the the non-human primates.

There can be no doubt that there is a great difference between the forms of communication found in the apes and man's use of language. The non-human primates seem to be capable of communicating only about very restricted numbers of events. Their forms of communication have no counterpart in the vocabulary, the phonology, and the grammar of language. One essential difference between their forms of communication and verbal communication seems to be that the signals they use have a restricted symbolic value.

If one assumes that the vocabulary, grammar, and phonology of a language make up an indivisible whole, and further that thinking is dependent upon language, it is difficult to imagine how language could evolve out of the primitive forms of communication found in the non-human primates. However, if one assumes—in line with what I have argued in the previous chapters—that the main parts of language are relatively loosely related to each other and that language is based upon highly developed intellective capacities, it is not so difficult to imagine that language has evolved in this way. As I shall argue in Chapter 7, names of objects and activities may be highly useful in communication even if they are used without grammatical rules. If one assumes that verbal communication began in the way that our ancestors acquired the use of a few names, it is not so difficult to imagine that the number of names may gradually have been extended to a sizable vocabulary, that rules for the use of the signs (grammatical rules) may gradually have been acquired, and that the mechanisms for the production of sounds may have been refined so as to allow the sounds produced to be related in a phonological system.

The step which is probably most difficult to understand is the one leading from the primitive forms of communication found in the non-human primate species to that of using names for communication. However, as I noted in Chapter 1, attempts at teaching names for the use of communication to chimpanzees suggest that under certain conditions they may learn to use names. This is an indication that the capacity for using names for communication may not be far above the capacities of chimpanzees. Therefore, while learning to use names may not be so simple as assumed by Osgood, Skinner, Mowrer, and other behaviourists of the 1950s and 60s, this learning may not be far beyond the capacities of the chimpanzees. Hence, even if it is not known how our ancestors acquired the use of names for communication, evidence suggests that the transition from the primitive forms of communication to communication based on the use of names, may have been more or less continuous. In the previous chapter I argued that language has a basis in perception and thinking, and that it is not possible to understand its nature unless this point is taken into account. However, the fact that language has a basis, a root, in thinking need not imply that it has evolved as a means of thinking. For two reasons it is not plausible to believe that language has evolved as a means of thinking. In the first place, it is difficult to understand what use our ancestors might have had for abstract symbols. As I pointed out in the previous chapter, prior to acquiring language, our ancestors were most likely capable of handling numerous tasks involving thinking. They were capable of identifying a large number of different objects and events and of establishing numerous associations between them. So, obviously they did not need words or grammar for representing relationships between objects and events. One must, therefore, ask what use they could possibly have had for abstract symbols? I think the belief that language originated as a means of thinking is only attractive if one assumes that our ancestors, prior to acquiring language, were *not* capable of handling tasks involving thinking.

The other reason for not believing that language originated in thinking, is that the abstract symbols which were to be used for thinking would be the private property of the individual having acquired them. This is so because the individuals acquiring the symbols were not capable of communicating with each other, because they had no language. To evolve into language, the symbols which each individual in a group possessed as private property had to be common to the members of the population. I think it is unlikely that the indivduals of a population should acquire an assembly of abstract symbols which they all came to share. It seems fair to conclude that it is not plausible to believe that language evolved as a means of thinking.

Communication is behaviour and when the primary function of language is communication, use of language must be classed as a form of behaviour. Up to the Second World War European psychologists and linguists tended one-sidedly to conceive of language as a mental phenomenon. As I emphasized in Chapter 1, it is to the credit of the behaviourists that they made clear that use of language is behaviour. However, in their eagerness to try to avoid reference to cognitive activities they lost sight of the fact that language has a basis in perception and thinking and that it is not possible to describe verbal behaviour without also using a terminology referring to these capacities. To deal in a fruitful manner with linguistic problems *research workers must treat language partly as a mental and partly as a behavioural phenomenon.*

Speaking and thinking are so closely related that one may easily come to confound the two activities and behaviourists and mentalists have tended to confound them and have thereby come to overlook essential characteristics of speech. Thinking goes on within an individual; it is a private affair. In contrast, verbal communication takes place between individuals; it is a social affair. Thinking may take place in an individual even if no other individual has made the thinker aware of what she or he is thinking about. The thinker may happen to perceive, remember, or imagine some object or event and may start thinking about this object or event. However, in order *to transmit information by means of language, speakers must direct the attention of other individuals to objects or events about which they want to communicate.* This marks an important difference between thinking and speaking. If this point is overlooked, a fundamental characteristic of language is left out of consideration.

In order to direct the attention of other individuals, speakers must do something which these individuals must be capable of registering. Hence, as I have already emphasized, verbal communication represents a specific type of behaviour and it is not possible to understand how information is transmitted unless this behaviour is taken into account. In other words, we shall not understand what is meant by speaking and listening if we regard the use of language as a process going on within an individual, i.e. as a private affair.

It is perfectly sensible to say, as Chomsky and generative grammarians do, that language is a set of internalized rules. However, unless it is made clear how individuals using these rules *behave* in order to direct the attention of other individuals, it is hardly possible to understand what can be meant by a rule for the use of language. Also, as I mentioned in Chapter 1, it is perfectly sensible to maintain, as Chomsky (1968), Lenneberg (1967), and Derek Bickerton (1981) do, that the capacity for using language is dependent upon some genetically determined mechanism, However, it is hardly possible to understand what can be meant by saying that the capacity for language is genetically determined, unless one has made clear how an individual capable of thinking is capable of communicating something to another individual. In their postulation of a genetic mechanism for the acquisition of language, the scientists mentioned seem to have overlooked the distinction between thinking and speaking, and, as I have shown, this distinction is probably of fundamental importance. Looking at language in a manner which seems to be highly similar to that of Chomsky, Jerrold Fodor (1976) suggested that thinking is a language. As I hope to have shown, by making this assumption one deprives language of an essential characteristic. Also, by making this assumption one meets with great difficulties in explainig how *thinking* has evolved in the evolution of the primate species.

In the previous chapter I emphasized that the communicatory acts in which the non-human primates engage are mainly expressions of emotions. However, this fact must not, as pointed out by Marler (1984), lead one to overlook that these acts have also a symbolic, a cognitive component. This follows from the fact that the emotional expressions are *social* in origin. They serve, as made clear by Washburn and Strum in the article referred to in the previous chapter, to regulate the social relationships of the individuals of a group. It is not possible to distinguish an affective or emotional component from a symbolic or cognitive component. According to Marler, in the further evolution of the primitive forms of communication the symbolic component has increased in importance. Hence, the belief that language has originated in communicatory acts which mainly express emotions, is not in opposition to the belief that language has a root in emotions. Apparently, unless it can be assumed that an emotional component can be separated from a cognitive component, one can infer that language has originated in emotions. What can be said is that language has a root in emotions.

However, even if one assumes that in primitive communicatory acts the two components are not distinguishable, one might still hold that language has originated as a means of *expressing* emotions. When it is considered that the non-human primates have a variety of effective means of expressing emotions this belief does not seem plausible. One might even hold that non-verbal means of expressing emotions, such as grimacing, taking postures, staring, moving eyes and limbs, grunting, wimpering, yelling, and caressing, are superior to verbal utterances. While it is important to realize that most likely language has a root in emotions, it is important to note that it is hardly plausible to believe that language originated as a means of expressing emotions.

What I have said about the belief that language may have originated in emotions, also seems to be relevant to the belief that language might have originated in phatic communion. As I have already mentioned, according to Malinowski 'phatic communion' is the use of language to make contact between individuals and to maintain stability of a group. Prior to acquiring language, our ancestors seem to have had a large variety of means for making contact and for maintaining stability in groups. Also, it should be noted that, according to Hymes (ibid), the use of language for the purposes described by Malinowski may not be universal. In other words, phatic communion may not play the central role ascribed to it by Malinowski. Still, I think it must be accepted that uses of language of the types described by Malinowski are not easily characterized as primarily involving a transmittance of information.

Having given my arguments for the belief that language originated as a means of communication, I shall show that it is possible to regard other uses of it as derived from that use.

The many uses of language

The first point I want to make concerns the traditional division of sentences into the three types: declarative, interrogative, and imperative sentences. It will be understood that all three types may contain utterances aimed at transmitting information. Information need not be transmitted only in the form of statements, assertions or descriptions, but may be transmitted also in the form of commands, instructions, advice, and exhortations. This means that imperative sentences also usually represent instances of transmittance of information. The type of sentence which most clearly brings to focus that language is a means of transmitting information is the interrogative sentence. In using this type of sentence speakers announce that they lack some specific item or type of information and the persons to whom the question is addressed try to provide them with this information. The ease with which speakers ask questions shows how deeply rooted the belief is that language is a means of transmitting information.

I shall turn to uses of language which are obviously dependent upon transmittance of information, but in which speakers may not have the specific intention of transmitting some item or type of information. When people tell stories and jokes they have to provide their listeners with information of various sorts. These uses of language are, therefore, clearly dependent upon the fact that information can be transmitted by means of language. It is natural to regard the telling of stories and jokes as activities which depend upon the fact that language is a means of transmitting information. If it were not, these uses would not be possible. The telling of stories and jokes may be regarded as derived from the fact that language can serve as a means of communication. A similar reasoning can be carried out for the fact that language can be used for telling lies. The person telling the lie takes the point of departure in the fact that listeners tend to assume that utterances addressed to them contain information. Hence, this function of language is dependent upon the fact that language is a means of transmitting information. Also, this use may be said to be derived from the fact that language is a means of communication. The fact that language can be used for telling stories, jokes, and lies may actually be regarded as strong evidence that the main function of language is communication.

There can be no doubt that people frequently use language to arouse emotions and that the *main* purpose of speakers and writers sometimes is to do so. It does not take much reflection to understand that the reason speakers and writers can use language in this way is that by means of language it is possible to provide types of information to which feelings and emotions of various kinds can be associated. Hence, the very fact that language can be used for the transmittance of information makes it possible to use it also for arousing emotions. So far I have considered uses of language which are not produced with the intention of transmitting some definite information, but which are based upon the fact that language is a means of communication. I shall now turn to uses in which the communicatory function is not so prominent. All languages seem to have words and phrases, such as the English, *Ah*, *Aha*, *Oh*, *Alas*, *Ouch*, *Hurrah*, *Heavens*, *Hell*, *Good gracious*, *What a pity*, to designate feelings and emotions in the speaker. It would be strained to say that their primary function is to transmit information. Furthermoore, there are phrases for greetings, for expressing politeness, and for maintaining contact. As I have already mentioned, Malinowski was right in maintaining that phrases, such as, *Good morning*, *How do you do*, *Nice to see you*, *Fine weather today*, *Farewell*, etc. are not uttered with the main intention of transmitting some definite information to another individual.

While it would be strained to say that the types of phrases listed above are primarily used to transmit information, it is also difficult to maintain that they are not communicatory acts. I think it is possible to argue that these expressions belong to language, but one might probably also hold that they should be classified with the non-verbal forms of human communication. It will be noted that verbal utterances of the type I am discussing can frequently be replaced by non-verbal acts, such as nodding, bowing, raising one's hand, shrugging one's shoulders, etc. They seem to lie on the borderline between verbal and non-verbal acts of communication. They represent a problem for the delimitation of a field of linguistic research, but, as I argued in the previous section, they can hardly be taken as an important argument against the belief that the primary function of language is communication.

In the previous section I emphasized that language has a root in perception and thinking, but that it is implausible that it has originated as a form of thinking. According to this way of looking at matters the use made of language in thinking must be regarded as derived from the function of communication. In the previous chapter I called attention to the fact that in our present state of knowledge it is difficult to explain how language enters into thinking. When account is taken also of this fact it will be understood that a reference to a possible use of language in thinking can hardly provide a decisive argument against the belief that the primary function of language is communication. When this possibility is excluded I do not think it is easy to find types of uses of language which show that its primary function is not communication. In this connection I want to mention that I am unable to see that in defending his extreme mentalist position Chomsky (1981) has been capable of presenting good arguments against the widely accepted belief that the primary function of language is communication. Whether the term 'information' is sufficiently precise to be used in productive research is a question which must be decided within the philosophy of science. I shall turn to that question in the next chapter.

Conclusion

There can be no doubt that language has many uses and it would be wrong to state that the only use of language is communication. However, the belief that language originated in communication and that other functions are derived from this use, is in agreement with present knowledge of the evolution of the primate species. Hence the intuition—of what probably represents a majority of students of language—that the primary function of language is communication, seems to rest on rather solid empirical evidence. However, due to the fact that language has so many uses, it is not easy to produce a precise definition of the term 'information'. In the previous chapter I pointed out that the term 'information' meets also with the difficulty that its use so easily entangles the research workers in subtle questions concerning consciousness. Still, in spite of the lacking precision of the term, I think it is sufficiently clear to allow research workers to deal with a variety of problems in a productive manner.

To say that the primary function of language is communication, is to say that the use of language is a form of behaviour. In Chapter 1 I mentioned that it is to the credit of the behaviourists that they called attention to the fact that use of language is behaviour, but that they have contributed very little to an understanding of that behaviour. In Chapter 7 I shall make an attempt at specifying what is characteristic of verbal behaviour. In that chapter I shall also discuss Austin's idea of how speakers perform, to which I referred in the beginning of the present chapter. I shall show that he overlooked an important aspect of verbal communication.

Chapter 4

Plan for the scientific study of language

Thus a premium is placed on the role of rationality in the growth of scientific knowledge—that premium being placed in large part in response to its absence in positivistic philosophy of science and its near absence in the work of Kuhn and Feyerabend. Further, contemporary work in philosophy of science increasingly subscribes to the position that it is a central aim of science to come to knowledge of how the world really is, that correspondence between theories and reality is a central aim of science as an epistemic enterprise and crucial to whatever objectivity scientific knowledge enjoys—in sharp repudiation of the "sociological" views of knowledge found in the more extreme Weltanschauungen analyses while acknowledging the defects of positivistic and earlier empiricist treatments. — — —.

Frederick Suppe, Afterword—1977, p. 649

The social sciences of the 20th century were dominated by positivist ideas of science and particularly the study of language seems to have been under this dominance. In a search for more useful ideas it is natural to begin by considering what now appear as the main deficiencies in positivist thinking about science. As the reader will know, the positivist ideas have come under strong attack from various quarters. Much of the criticism has been summed up in a detailed, systematic and penetrating exam nation of the beliefs of the logical positivists undertaken by Frederick Suppe (1982). I shall repeat some of the main points in this criticism.

Positivist conceptions of science

A characteristic of positivist thinking about science is that speculation should be avoided. This led the positivists to emphasize inductive procedures. As F. A. Chalmers (1984) has pointed out, some of them—referred to as the naive inductivists—had no place for creative ideas in the scientific procedure. Chalmers (1984, p. 5) characterized their attitude to science in the following way:

> According to the naive inductivist, then, the body of scientific knowledge is built by induction from the secure basis provided by observation. As the number of facts established by observation and experiment grows, and as the facts become more refined and esoteric due to improvements in our observational and experimental skills, so more and more laws and theories of ever more generality and scope are constructed by careful inductive reasoning. The growth of science is continuous, ever onward and upward, as the fund of observational data is increased.

In the version of positivism originating with Ernst Mach, and which became the dominant one, observations were accorded a fundamental role in theory construction. Observations in the form of sensory impressions came to be regarded as the rock bottom of the scientific structure. Mach was followed by the members of the Vienna Circle, the logical positivists. They realized that Mach and the earlier positivists had one-sidedly emphasized inductive procedures and thus had overlooked the role played by deductions and creative ideas in science. They tried to remove this defect in the earlier positivist thinking by conceiving of scientific theories as axiomatic systems and thus of systems which allowed for deductions. By noting whether or not the deductions agreed with observations scientists might, so it was thought, test their theories. They claimed there were three kinds of terms in the scientific system: 1. logical and mathematical terms, 2. theoretical terms, and 3. observational terms. By so-called correspondence rules the theoretical terms were believed to be related to the observational terms.

The logical positivists drew a rigid distinction between theoretical and observational terms. By maintaining this distinction they could argue that scientific theories might be justified by relatively simple procedures. If a theory had an appropriate logical structure, derivations might be made from it and the derivations compared to actual observations. Now, if the distinction between theoretical and observational terms is not so clear-cut as believed by the positivists, science cannot have the firm foundation in observations, and this elegant and simple procedure breaks down. Philosophers of science, such as Karl Popper (1934), Norwood

Hanson (1958), Thomas Kuhn (1962), Stephen Toulmin (1963), Paul Feyerabend (1975), and Dudley Shapere (1977), have pointed to difficulties in drawing the distinction and most modern philsophers of science will agree with Suppe's (ibid, p. 68) conclusion that the observational-theoretical distinction is untenable.

According to modern philosophers of science theories are typically not developed by subjecting them to the kind of tests suggested by the positivists. As pointed out by Suppe (ibid, p. 706), scientists working on a theory usually suppose that it is defective and thus literally false and they use observation and experiment to discover shortcomings in the formulations:

> And when one looks at how observation and experiment are employed in evaluating sophisticated theories within these larger units, one finds that the focus typically is not what philosophers of science have characterized as inductively confirming a theory as true or refuting it as false. When a sophisticated theory is undergoing active development, it is commonplace for scientists working on it to suppose that the present version of the theory is defective in various respects, which is to say that it is literally false, at best being only an approximation to the truth or a promising candidate, and if one is convinced this is so, it would be pointless to attempt to either refute or inductively confirm the theory. What *is* to the point is to use observation and experiment to discover shortcomings in the theory, to determine how to improve the theory, and to discover how to eliminate known artificialities, distortions, oversimplifications, and errors in the descriptions, explanations, and predictions of reality that the theory affords.

Frequently it is difficult to understand more precisely what is implied by the statements contained in theoretical models depicting complicated phenomena. If one could construct the model as an axiomatic system, as a calculus, one might derive consequences from the axioms and in this way find out what is implied by the theoretical statements. Hence, as suggested by the logical postivists, by formulating a theory as an axiomatic system, one might produce a refined and elegant procedure for determing implications of theoretical statements. Unfortunately, for two good reasons this procedure is hardly an efficient one. In the first place, as pointed out by Shapere (ibid) and Toulmin (ibid), in most scientific systems one finds logical gaps and inconsistencies and it is precisely these gaps and inconsistencies which keep a subject alive. Secondly, as concluded by Suppe (ibid, p. 64), unless the relationships between theoretical concepts are well understood, fruitful axiomatization is not possible:

> For such fruitful axiomatization to be possible, rather extensive knowledge of the interconnections between the component concepts of the pre-axiomatic theory must be on hand. The axiomatic method in effect is a method for introducing order into an already well-developed body of knowledge; in particular fruitful axiomatization of a theory is possible only if the theory to be axiomatized embodies a well-developed body of knowledge for which the systematic interconnections of its concepts are understood to a high degree. Without these conditions being met, any attempt at axiomatization will be premature and fruitless.

In connection with the point made by Suppe it should be noted that in the study of language—and in general in the social sciences—relationships between concepts are usually poorly understood. Therefore, in these sciences work devoted to axiomatizations of theories will probably be unproductive.

The positivists believed that scientists might avoid dealing with metaphysical questions. However, as made clear by Rom Harré (1972), the choice of concepts in terms of which scientists have decided to carry out their thinking involves metaphysical beliefs:

> I hope it has become clear that philosophical problems are assumed in any scientific practice. We have to choose some concepts with which to think about the world, and this amounts to devising or learning a language, and accepting a system of picturing and conceiving the structures in the world. Any set of concepts we choose, no matter how much they may lack systematic connection, involves metaphysical, epistemological, and logical assumptions (p. 16).

Hence, to develop an appropriate approach to the study of a phenomenon, it is necessary to undertake a careful examination of the metaphysical beliefs which underly its conceptions.

In connection with the point made by Harré it should be noted that the choice of concepts on which to base a scientific study involves an evaluation of metaphysical beliefs as to their appropriateness to the task confronting the scientists. As Lila Gleitman and Eric Wanner (1982, p. 42) have emphasized, beliefs must be evaluated with regard to their appropriateness as a basis for the theory to be constructed:

> At the very bottom of any scientific paradigm lies a set of beliefs that are usually called metaphysical. It is sometimes claimed that these deep beliefs about the nature of theories and the things they

> describe cannot be confirmed or disconfirmed by empirical means. It is, however, quite possible to compare different metaphysical beliefs according to the degree of success of the scientific programs they support. Moreover, substantive arguments for one set of metaphysical assumptions over others can be constructed on this basis.

In this discussion I have considered some of the tenets of positivism. Suppe undertook, as I have already mentioned, a systematic and comprehensive examination of the ideas advanced by the logical positivists. In a chapter entitled "Swansong for positivism" he concluded "that virtually the whole positivistic program for philosophy of science has been repudiated by contemporary philosophy of science" (Suppe, ibid, p. 632).

The social sciences were strongly affected by positivist ideas about science. For example, positivism prepared the ground for behaviourism and was responsible for its enthusiastic acceptance by American psychologists. The study of language as it is being carried out by linguists of the twentieth century seems to be a product of positivist thinking about science. Linguists take their point of departure in the utterances speakers make in their particular languages. One may ask: Why should the scientific study of language take this specific point of departure? Admittedly, it may be said that it is a fact about speech that it contains utterances. However, it is also a fact that speech is carried on within speech communities and a fact about speech that it is a form of communication. Why take the point of departure from the utterances which speakers make in their particular languages? I think it is difficult to give a good answer to this question. The reason why linguists have taken this point of departure is probably to be found in the fact that according to positivist thinking all sciences have a firm foundation in observation. The utterances made by speakers in their particular languages might be observed. Having established what they believed to be a solid foundation for the study of language, linguists would proceed to theory construction either by way of inductive procedure or by introducing models which accounted for the utterances. Bloomfield may be seen as a representative of the first and Chomsky as a representative of the second course. In other words, positivism in its early version was adopted by Bloomfield and positivism in the version of the logical positivists by Chomsky. In a well known passage in the introductory chapter to his influential textbook Bloomfield (1934) wrote: "The only useful generalizations about language are inductive generalizations". Bloomfield seems to come very close to fitting the description which Chalmers gave of the naive inductivist. Chomsky (1957, p. 49) gave the following statement of his position to the role played by the utterances made by speakers in a scientific study of language:

> Our fundamental concern throughout this discussion of linguistic structure is the problem of justification of grammars. A grammar of the language L is essentially a theory of L. Any scientific theory is based on a finite number of observations, and it seeks to relate the observed phenomena and to predict new phenomena by constructing general laws in terms of hypothetical constructs such as (in physics, for example) "mass" and "electron". Similarly, a grammar of English is based on a finite corpus of utterances (observations), and it will contain certain grammatical rules (laws) stated in terms of the particular phonemes, phrases, etc., of English (hypothetical constructs). These rules express structural relations among the sentences of the corpus and the indefinite number of sentences generated by the grammar beyond the corpus (predictions). Our problem is to develop and clarify the criteria for selecting the correct grammar for each language, that is, the correct theory of this language.

Evidently linguists have based their approaches upon the positivist belief that science has a firm basis in observations.

The criticism made of positivism by modern philosophers of science strongly suggests that scientists must look for alternatives to positivism if they want to develop productive procedures for their fields of research. I shall consider what appears as a promising alternative.

An alternative to positivism

An alternative to positivism has been presented by Shapere (ibid) and Suppe (ibid). Reacting to the drawing of a distinction between observational and theoretical terms Shapere suggested that the point of departure should be taken in the idea of a domain. A 'domain' is a body of related items of information. It consists of beliefs which the theorist regards as well established (as facts) and of beliefs which on further research the theorist assumes will prove to be facts (so-called putative facts). The facts and putative facts are referred to as the items of the domain. In Shapere's reasoning it is important that for something to be a domain the ordering of the items must represent a problem. As I have mentioned, Shapere reacted to the drawing of a sharp line of division between observational and theoretical terms. It should be noted that to him a fact is not an observation in terms of some sensory impression. A fact may be any well founded belief and it may even be a theory. As underlined by Shapere, what at some stage in empirical research may be regarded as a fact may at some earlier stage have had the status of theory.

According to Shapere, theories are developed in the attempts of scientists to solve the problems raised by their conceptions of their domains. In terms of this idea he has given an inspiring account of the development of various areas of physics. He has shown that in their attempts at ordering domains, scientists seem to apply definite reasoning patterns, and that as research progresses these patterns become tighter.

By rejecting the belief that scientific theories have a firm basis in observations Shapere is free to consider all types of information or knowledge as forming the basis for theory construction. This, I think, gives a more realistic picture of what is involved in scientific theory construction. Also, by including in the basic structure beliefs which theorists believe may prove to be facts (putative facts), he obtains a more flexible approach to problems of theory construction. As it is well known, what at one time scientists may regard as a mere plausibility, they may at a later stage hold to be a fact, and what at one time they may regard as a fact, they may at a later time consider to be an accidental property of some phenomenon. Having taken the point of departure in a specified set of items of information (facts and putative facts) Shapere can proceed to conceive of the task of theory construction as that of ordering the items.

The idea of a domain is not, of course, unproblematic. In the first place the idea presupposes that the items are related to each other. In other words, in order to take the point of departure in the idea of a domain the scientists must have some idea of an order among the items. Toulmin (1963) has shown the great role ideas of an existing order play in theory construction. Secondly, in order for something to represent a domain, the ordering of the items must, according to Shapere, represent a problem. Apparently attempts at ordering a set of items may raise a variety of problems and one may wonder whether this requirement to the definition of a domain adds anything of importance. If this requirement is left out, the use of the term 'domain' seems more or less to correspond to the more frequently used terms 'field' or 'area of research', and I shall use the latter terms. The difference between a field and an area of research I shall take to be that a field is frequently divided into a number of sub-areas.

In line with the considerations presented above I shall say that at an initial stage theory construction may be said to have two main aspects. The first one concerns the specification of the items (facts and putative facts) to be included in the field or area of research and the second the ordering of items included in the field or area. The two aspects of theory construction are closely related to each other. A new way of ordering a field may lead to the inclusion of new items or to the exclusion of items originally included in the field of research, and the inclusion or exclusion of some item may lead to a new ordering of the field. Actually decisions as to what should be regarded as facts in a field of research cannot be determined without considering how beliefs assumed to represent facts are related to available theories in the field. Elsewhere (Saugstad, 1989) I have discussed the problem which arises because facts and theories are so closely related to each other.

The first aspect may be described as that of preparing a list of items to be included in the field of research. To prepare this list theorists must undertake an examination of beliefs assumed to be relevant for an understanding of the phenomenon to be investigated. This examination must be undertaken with a view to deciding whether the beliefs under consideration are plausible, and whether there is a choice between alternative beliefs, which may be more plausible. Having performed this examination theorists must decide which of the beliefs considered should be included as items of the field of research. Also, they must decide which of the beliefs they regard as facts, and to which they will attribute the status of being putative facts. The procedure is merely a refinement of a type of reasoning people carry out in many everyday life situations and has probably been followed by scientists for centuries. However, under the dominance of positivist thinking about science the belief seems to have become widespread that theory construction at its initial stages can proceed by simpler and more efficient methods. No such methods seem to exist.

By their choice of items to be included in the field of research theorists have indicated what they believe to represent the reality to be studied. It should be noted that as research progresses new items will be included and some items originally included will be excluded. In other words, the conception of the reality studied undergoes more or less continuous changes. From historical studies of physics it is known that over time the physicists' conceptions of reality have changed. Changes in conceptions of the reality studied are, therefore, to be expected. What I have referred to as the first aspect in my procedure may be regarded as a preparatory way of delimiting a field and I shall also refer to it as the 'delimitation of the field of research'.

At early stages of theory construction, the choice of items to be included in a field of research may easily become affected by subjective factors. Because there are no effective methods for dealing with problems regarding this choice, it is to be expected that at initial stages of theory construction scientists will tend to disagree as to what should be regarded as the items of the field. In this connection it should be mentioned that studies undertaken by Kuhn (ibid) of the history of various areas of physics, reveal that at early stages of research scientists have difficulties reaching consensus concerning formulations of problems. These difficulties become understandable when it is noted that at these stages scientists tend to disagree on the choice of items to be included in their areas of research.

The second aspect, the ordering of the items of the field, consists in specifying and investigating relationships between the items with a view to accounting for the facts and the putative facts in a way which is as coherent and consistent as possible. The account given of the items is the theory, and to give this account scientists have to construct a model which pictures the reality studied. In attempts at accounting for the items of a field of research theorists usually have to hold some definite beliefs concerning certain relationships. This frequently requires certain items to be explained. For this reason it is usually not possible to give an adequate account of the items of a field of research merely by describing the items and their relationships. Useful theoretical models must contain explanations of certain beliefs.

Apparently, in a field containing a number of items and numerous relationships between them, it is difficult to obtain a picture of the relationships. As an aid to obtaining this picture scientists frequently search for ideas which may help them to integrate the field. Toulmin (1963) has shown that ideas of a general order may play a great role in attempts at advancing a field or area of research. Norman Cambell (1921) pointed out that many scientific theories contain an idea which help scientists to conceive of certain events or phenomena in analogy with other types of events. He even argued that a scientific theory must contain an analogy. (For a discussion of this claim, see John Losee, 1980.) Without going into his argument I shall hold that ideas in the form of analogies may be highly useful in attempts at constructing scientific theories. At initial stages in theory construction at which relationships between items tend to be obscure, it may even be necessary to try to integrate a field by introducing ideas which help scientists to conceive of certain phenomena in analogy with other phenomena. Elsewhere (Saugstad, 1989) in a discussion of procedures in the study of psychology I have argued that unless social scientists start out with some overall idea of the phenomenon they want to study, it is difficult to understand how they can proceed by deductive as well as inductive methods. An example of the role which overall ideas may play in the development of a field of research is the idea of biological evolution introduced by Charles Darwin and Alfred Russell Wallace. In terms of this idea the study of biology was revolutionized. Another idea by Darwin which has organized a field of research is the idea that man has descended from individuals of an earlier existing primate species. In Chapter 2 I mentioned how the study of the evolution of man was organized around this idea, and in Chapter 1 I argued that the study of phonology might be conceived of as based upon the idea that phonemes have the function of forming morphemes which can be discriminated from each other. In line with the role which I think must be attributed to overall ideas in scientific research, I shall introduce an idea which may help integrate linguistic research. The task ahead of me can be described as that of developing this idea into a theoretical model.

The more coherent, consistent, and simple a theory is, the more useful and satisfactory it is. However, there can be no such thing in science as absolute standards. Theories can only be as good as current knowledge allows them to be. This means that no clear lines can be drawn between science and general cultural knowledge. Theoretical concepts can only be as precise as circumstances allow them to be. The same is true of the relationships between the concepts. Nor can there be a standard for deciding how adequately a theory ought to account for the facts. Actually few—if any—theories can account for all facts.

In the advanced sciences research workers try to express as many relationships as possible in terms of mathematical systems. This allows them to treat relationships between items in a manner which is enormously more productive than treatments of relationships merely in terms of verbal statements. One might, therefore, think that the most appropriate way of advancing a field is to introduce quantitative measures. However, when the relationships between the items are obscure it is to be doubted that much can be achieved by introducing quantification and mathematics. Apparently, as I think it is evidenced in the advancement of biology, great progress may be achieved by slow and careful investigation of relationships between items which are expressed without the use of quantification and mathematics. When relationships become better understood a time may come when these powerful tools can be introduced.

To develop an idea so that it can account for the relationships between items assumed to be contained in a field, theorists have to take a stand on numerous empirical issues. They must show that what they have regarded as putative facts actually are facts. Relationships between the items must be specified and some of the relationships postulated must be explained. A theory may be useful because it can explain a specific relationship, but ordinarily the usefulness of a theory is due to the fact that it allows scientists to conceive of the items as an integrated whole. It will be understood that the value of such a theory is not dependent upon the fact that it has withstood particular tests. Actually, it is rarely possible to subject a theory to a crucial test. As I mentioned in the discussion of positivism, this is also the conclusion arrived at by modern philosophers of science.

The testing of a theory probably becomes important when another theory has emerged which seems to account equally well for the facts. To decide which theory is to be preferred the two theories must be subjected to specific tests. In the history of the physical sciences the testing of rival theories has presented particularly dramatic events, and this may have led philosophers to attach undue emphasis to the role played by tests in theory construction. As I have pointed out, and as was made clear by Suppe in the quotation given on page 69, scientists are concerned mainly with the improvement of existing theories and not with the problem of refuting them.

As philosophers of science have shown, it always seems possible to account for a set of facts in more than one way. Hence, scientific theories must in some sense be the constructions of the minds of the theorists. However, this fact must not lead one to overlook that the constructions are constrained by the fact that scientists are confronted with the task of accounting for a variety of different facts. The logical positivists as well as their contemporary colleague Popper seem to have overemphasized the freedom scientists have in constructing theories. Popper (1963, p. 117) gave the following explicit statement of his position when he wrote: "Theories are our own inventions, our own ideas; they are not forced upon us, but are our own self-made instruments of thought; this has been clearly seen by the idealist." It must be admitted that it is extremely difficult to give a satisfactory account of how scientific theories reflect the reality studied. But when account is taken of the fact that in constructing their theories scientists have to take a stand on a large variety of different types of knowledge, it would be strange indeed if their constructions should be the theorists' own inventions. Apparently Popper tended to overlook that any field of empirical research contains a number of facts which scientists must account for. This oversight led Popper to place an undue emphasis on the role played by the testing of theories.

Procedure

In the previous chapter I argued that theory construction in fields not yet structured by theory has two essential aspects. One concerns the delimitation of the field and the other the ordering of the field.

Delimitation of a field of linguistic research. The first aspect I described as that of preparing a list of facts and putative facts which the theorist believes ought to be included in the field. I shall prepare a list of items which I think should be included in a field of linguistic research. I shall regard it as a fact about language that it is a means of communication, a means of transmitting information from one individual to another. However, I shall not regard it as an indisputable fact that communication is the primary function of language. The latter belief I shall regard as a putative fact. In Chapter 3 I discussed this belief.

Apparently, in order that an individual shall be capable of transmitting information to another individual, the two individuals must perform, behave, in some manner. In other words, if language is regarded as a means of communication the use of it must be a form of behaviour, and I shall regard it as a fact that use of language is a form of behaviour.

As a form of behaviour use of language need not have evolved because this function is a result of biological adaptation. However, I think it is highly plausible to believe that it has evolved in this way and I shall regard it as a putative fact that language has an adaptive biological function.

Further, I shall regard it as a fact that the capacity for language has a close relationship to cognitive capacities, such as perceiving, remembering, imagining, and thinking. By this type of close relationship I have in mind that it is not possible to account for verbal communication unless assumptions are made concerning cognitive capacities such as those mentioned. However, I shall not regard it as a fact that in some way language is a means of expressing thoughts. This I shall regard as a putative fact. In Chapter 2 I presented arguments for this belief. As I made clear in Chapter 1, in attempts at delimiting language it is essential that scientists make clear whether or not they want to include thinking in their field of research.

In addition to the types of facts listed above there are the facts established by the comparative research of the linguists. In Chapter 1, I pointed out that linguists have shown that in the speech of all people one finds three different types of elements: 1. discrete signs having definite meanings, 2. sentences consisting of combinations of the discrete signs, 3. elementary sounds combined according to various rules to make up the signs of the language. In Chapter 1 I also listed as an important fact established by linguists that although the structure of the languages of the world differs in a number of respects, they are all highly efficient means of communication. No primitive language has been found.

There is also a third type of facts about language. This concerns the acquisition of language in the course of the ontogenetic development. Children begin talking by using one or a few signs. These signs resemble the words found in the speech of the adults making up the speech community of the children. The first utterances produced typically consist of one single sign. As I mentioned in Chapter 1, it is natural to regard these utterances as one-word utterances. At a somewhat later stage children typically produce utterances consisting of two signs in juxtaposition (two-word utterances). Furthermore, as in the subsequent development the number of words increases, the child gradually learns to use grammatical rules for the formation of sentences. Along with the acquisition of a vocabulary and the use of grammatical rules there is a gradual improvement in pronunciation, in the mastering of the phonological system.

Finally I shall mention a fourth type of facts, namely facts concerning individual variations in speech. Not only do different cultural groups speak different languages, but also within cultural groups which are highly homogeneous one may find individual variations with regard to vocabulary, pronunciation, and use of grammatical principles.

Many scientists have held that language is a means of thinking, but no one seems to have been able to construct a theory either of thinking or of language, which makes it understandable that language can have this function. For this reason, and in spite of the fact that I believe it is plausible that language is a means of thinking, I shall not regard this as a putative fact, in other words I shall not include it in the postulated field. In Chapter 2 I discussed the effect of language upon thinking.

By listing the facts and putative facts in the way I have done above I have delimited the field to be investigated. I have postulated a field for linguistic research. The field postulated represents the reality to be studied. Earlier in the present chapter I pointed out that as empirical research produces new facts and as new putative facts are suggested, the reality studied undergoes changes. Hence, the field, the reality studied, is not to be conceived of as unchangeable. In line with this way of looking at matters, it is to be expected that the conceptions of the field I have postulated will also undergo changes as research progresses.

In the previous section I pointed out that at an initial stage of theory contruction scientists will tend to disagree as to what should be regarded as facts and putative facts. The delimitation of the field I have suggested raises a number of problems. In my judgement the most important of these problems concerns the relationship between thinking and language. I have assumed that thinking and language are separable, and I shall also assume that language has a basis in thinking. As I noted in Chapter 2, these beliefs run counter to central beliefs in linguistics and analytic philosophy. As I emphasized in Chapter 1, beliefs concerning the relationship between thinking and language underlie the approach scientists take to a number of important linguistic problems .

The ordering of the facts and putative facts in the field of linguistic research. In the previous section I suggested that to bring order into a field of research it may be useful—and even necessary—to introduce an idea which allows scientists to view the field as an integrated whole. Below I shall suggest an idea which I believe is useful in attempts at integrating linguistic research and I shall indicate how I think the idea can be developed into a comprehensive theoretical model of language and its use. Before I proceed I shall draw attention to the fact that an integration of the items I have listed for a field of linguistic research represents a task far more comprehensive than that of constructing a grammar, which shows how various types of elements are combined into sentences. The task is one of accounting for the possibility of transmitting information from one individual to another by means of grammatical sentences.

In my criticism of the linguists' conception of language I pointed out that they had made an arbitrary distinction between the structure and the function of language. I argued that structure and function must be regarded as two aspects of the same phenomenon and that light must be shed on structure by a study of function and vice versa. To achieve a more adequate conception of language an idea is needed which allows scientists to combine structure and function. An idea which allows them to perform this combination is the old assumption that language is an instrument and I shall regard language as such an instrument.

I listed as a fact that language is a means of communication and as a putative fact that communication is its primary function. In accordance with these two beliefs I shall say that language is an instrument for communication. In the list of items I have assumed to be contained in the field of linguistic research I included as a putative fact that language is a means of expressing thoughts. I shall take account of this item by saying that language is an instrument for the expression of thoughts in communication. By conceiving of language as an instrument for communication it will be noted that it may be possible to account for the putative fact that language forms part of an adaptive biological function.

To show that language is an instrument it is, of course, also necessary to account for the facts about language established by linguists. Apparently, in order to serve as a means of communication, the type of elements which are to be considered as the instrument must have meaning. This implies that the instrument must be either the sentence or the type of elements I have designated by the term 'linguistic sign'. The sentence is the unit of speech. Hence, if the linguistic sign is chosen as the instrument, an explanation must be given of how the linguistic sign can be the instrument while the sentence is the unit of speech. On the other hand, if the sentence is taken to be the instrument, it must be regarded also as the unit of meaning. This raises the problem of how sentences can obtain meaning independently of the linguistic signs which make up the sentences. If the sentence obtains its meaning because the linguistic signs have meaning, it is natural to regard the linguistic sign as the instrument. I think it is easier to give an explanation of how the linguistic sign can be the instrument while the sentence is the unit of speech, than to give an explanation of how sentences obtain meaning independently of the linguistic signs of which they are built up. Consequently *I shall regard the linguistic sign as the instrument.*

In Chapter 1 I pointed out that not all types of morphemes seem to be equally important in verbal communication. Words seem to be far more important than the other types of morphemes, and I shall maintain that the word is the instrument. As I mentioned in Chapter 1, I shall use the term 'word' in the sense of a 'lexeme'. Because there are many types of words, instead of saying that language is an instrument, I shall say that it is an *assembly of instruments.*

By characterizing language as an assembly of instruments I have said something about its structure. To give a more complete picture of the structure I shall have to explain how words obtain their meaning. To do so I shall have to discuss problems concerning the structure of perception and knowledge. I shall deal with these problems in Chapter 5 and shall suggest two principles which state how man's knowledge is organized. In Chapter 6 I shall discuss how I think words can be defined with reference to this organization, and I shall formulate two more principles, which state how they obtain their meaning.

Having accounted for what I believe to be an essential feature of the structure of language as an assembly of instruments, I shall turn to the problem of explaining how instruments with the structure indicated, can function as a means of communication. To formulate this explanation I shall take my point of departure in the fact that the transmittance of information from a speaker to a listener is a result of a cooperation between the two. This cooperation aims at, I shall say, adjusting differences in knowledge between the speaker and the listener, and this makes it possible to state what are the goals of speaker and listener. In Chapter 7 I shall discuss the goals of speaker and listener and proceed to formulate a fundamental principle of communication (my fifth principle). In terms of this principle and the four principles referred to above, I shall account for verbal communication.

A central point in my account of verbal communication is that by noting possible differences in knowledge, the speaker and the listener derive cues which guide their interaction. To derive information from a verbal utterance listeners use such cues. According to this way of looking at verbal communication, the information which listeners obtain from the utterances of the speaker is a result not only of the meaning of the linguistic signs contained in the sentences produced, but it is also a result of the cues listeners have for the interpretation of the utterance. Following this line of reasoning *the sentence must be regarded as the unit of information. It is a product of the use made of language, but it does not form part of language.*

As the reader will remember, Saussure thought the word came closest to being the unit of language. My position has in common with that of Saussure's that I regard the word as central and do not include the sentence in language. However, I shall not regard the word as the unit of language. The word—and in general the linguistic sign—I shall hold is the unit of meaning in verbal communication. Moreover, for reasons I made clear in Chapter 1, I shall reject the idea that language is a system of signs.

From what I said above, the term 'sentence' cannot be defined with reference only to the linguistic signs out of which it is composed. To define it, reference must also be made to the way information is transmitted in verbal communication. In Chapter 7 I shall in some greater detail discuss the nature of the sentence. In that chapter I shall argue that grammatical rules are rules for making verbal communication more efficient. In connection with the discussion of the nature of the sentence I shall also discuss the nature of the linguistic signs which are not words.

The third type of facts, facts about the ontogenetic development, which I have included in the field of research can be reconciled with the idea that language is an instrument. If words are the instuments, it is natural to believe that the child will begin verbal communication by making utterances consisting of one word only, that it next will proceed to combine two words, and finally combine words into sentences. The fourth type of fact can be accounted for by the idea that language is an instrument. Speakers will shape their instruments differently and will use them differently. This may explain the differences in speech found between individuals and between groups of individuals.

In order to develop into a comprehensive model the idea that language is an assembly of instruments I shall have to examine a number of beliefs to find out whether they are plausible or not, and, if there is a choice between two or more beliefs, to find out which is the more plausible. This examination raises a number of problems, some of which belong to philosophy's eternal issues. My examination does not, of course, aim at giving a satisfactory and final solution to the problems met with in selecting a set of beliefs on which to rest my model. If some of the problems raised by the examination can be solved, the foundation on which the model rests will be more secure. However, the solidity of the model is mainly a result of the way the various beliefs are related to each other. If the model can give a coherent and consistent account of the facts and putative facts assumed to be contained in the field of linguistic research, it has considerable solidity. If other scientists can make the model more coherent and consistent its solidity will be increased. In contrast to the positivists I do not look for a firm basis on which to rest my theory. As I have stated elsewhere (Saugstad, 1980), the art of science is to weave together weak strains of evidence into a solid fabric. It is primarily, I believe, by combining a number of plausible beliefs that science has produced its results.

Chapter 5

Categorisation and the structure of knowledge

We do not wish to oversimplify complex psychological processes, but we believe that the separability of perceptual properties is the fact that should be emphasized in a psychological account of linguistic categorizing and labeling.

George Miller and Philip Johnson-Laird, *Language and Perception*, p. 13

In Chapter 3 I rejected the belief that thinking and language are inseparable. I argued that language has a basis in understanding and thinking. In this chapter I shall examine man's understanding with a view to disclosing this basis. The idea I shall pursue is that man's understanding has a structure which is fundamental in the sense that it is not possible to account for cognition unless this structure is assumed.

Some of the questions I am going to examine belong to philosophy's eternal issues. This fact suggests that they can probably not be given entirely satisfactory answers. I shall search for answers which seem plausible and which provide a basis for understanding how the ordinary speaker of language is capable of determining the meaning of words. Some of the questions I am going to deal with are metaphysical questions. I am bringing up this point because I shall take a metaphysical position which seems to differ from that taken by many modern logicians to some of the questions I am going to examine. The logicians have dominated the modern discussion of these questions, it may therefore be clarifying to indicate what is the difference. Dummett (1967) contrasted the position of Frege to that of Descartes and lined him up with Aristotle and the Scholastics maintaining that "for Frege as for them logic was the beginning of philosophy" and that epistemology is not prior to any other branch of philosophy. Since Frege took this position Dummett regarded him as the first modern philosopher. Of course, no clear line of division can be established between logic and epistemology. Still Dummett may have pointed to an important difference in orientation to philosophical questions. In discussing perception, thinking, and meaning I shall take the position that in order to understand what is the basis of language one shall have to start out with an examination of how the world appears to us. To avoid misunderstandings I want to make clear that I do not believe that problems in the study of perception can be solved simply by appeals to phenomenological descriptions, but I believe that unless we pay close attention to such descriptions we shall never get problems of cognition and language right. In my judgement Frege and many of the most influential modern philosophers on problems of meaning have overlooked essential points in their descriptions of the perceptual world. I shall make two points which I think are essential and which I think have been overlooked. These two points I shall introduce by examining an instance of perception.

I shall examine a scene in which we perceive a physical object, a material body, say, a tree. In agreement with Gestalt psychologists I shall hold that human individuals do not see an aggregate of colours and shapes, not an aggregate of sensations, but an object which has a unity, which is a whole, a Gestalt. I shall also hold that what we see is an object of a definite kind, namely an object of the kind 'tree'. The point I am going to make is that what we see—or in general what we perceive—are *objects of definite kinds*. I shall formulate this important point in a more general manner and say that what we perceive is the member of a class; it belongs to a category. According to this position the only particulars we perceive and think of are specific instances of some definite category. Another way of stating the point is to say that what we perceive and think of is not perceived or thought of unless it is attributed to some definite category. In our thinking we may attribute something to more than one category, but we never perceive or think of something without attributing it to some category.

The point I have made here is easily overlooked because we are usually capable of attributing what we perceive to a number of different categories. For example, the tree we perceive we may attribute to the category 'plant' or the category 'material', 'object'. This fact may erroneously lead us to believe that at some point we perceive something which is *not* of some definite kind. Of course, we may take the metaphysical position that ultimately the world is made up of particulars which are *not* the members of specific categories, but as I shall show in this chapter this may unnecessarily complicate the account we give of language and meaning. I think it is simpler to assume that what we perceive and think of and consequently what we speak of belongs to definite categories. This frees us of the burden of accounting for the general, for the universal.

According to this way of looking at matters we may say that what we perceive and think of has meaning in the sense that it forms part of a category. I shall hold that we do not perceive or think of anything unless it has meaning. Because, as I concluded in Chapter 3, perception and thinking are not governed by language, I shall say that meaning resides in perception and thinking and in order to account for meaning we shall have to account for the structure of perception and thinking. It follows from this position that the study of semantics must take its point of departure in conceptions of perception and thinking and not in conceptions of linguistic structure. *Until we have understood how perception and thinking are structured we shall not understand semantical problems.*

The second point I shall make concerns the relationships between categories. This leads into the eternal philosophical question: What is meant by a concept? As we all know, concepts are related to each other. For example, the concept 'tree' is related to the concepts 'leaf', 'branch', 'trunk', 'root'. To have an understanding of what is meant by a tree we must have an understanding also of the other concepts mentioned. Attempts at accounting for the relationship between concepts raise a problem which I do not think has a definite solution. Instead of trying to solve it, I shall try to show that it is possible to give a satisfactory account of the nature of language without first presenting an adequate solution to it. However, to show that this is possible I shall have to discuss some of the questions raised in attempts at accounting for concepts. I shall show that from the fact that we cannot account satisfactorily for the nature of concepts it does not follow, as apparently believed by some modern philosophers, that the idea of concepts must be abandoned.

The scientific study of cognition may be formulated as that of accounting for the categories into which man's experience or knowledge is organized. This account would have to specify how the diverse categories are related to each other. The scientific study of cognition which originated around 1850 in the study of perception has merely made a beginning towards accounting for the categories into which man's knowledge is organized. It is essential that linguists and logicians studying the problem of meaning make a study of the history of the scientific investigation of perception and I shall take my point of departure in a consideration of assumptions underlying this study. However, it is also important to note that the scientific study of cognition is only in its beginning and that the knowledge on which scientists can base a study of semantics is very limited. This means that what at present can be said about semantical problems is highly limited. I shall emphasize that I am not going to present a theory of semantics. The points I am going to make may help to make clear how semantical problems might be studied scientifically. But my main reason for making them is that they may help to understand the basis language has in perception and thinking.

I shall begin by discussing the problem of accounting for the particular and the general and shall then turn to the problem of accounting for the relationship between categories.

The particular and the universal in perception and thinking

The problem of accounting for the relationship between the particular and the general belongs to philosophy's eternal issues. As the reader will remember, Aristotle was dissatisfied with the answer given to the question by Plato and ever since philosophers have debated the issue. Plato seems to have held that what ultimately exists are universals. In contrast Aristotle seems to have assumed that what ultimately exists are individual things. The problem of the nature of the universal was central in the theological and philosophical discussions of medieval thinkers. It emerged in the philosophical systems of John Locke, George Berkeley and David Hume who seem to have assumed that perception is ultimately of particulars, i.e. that in some ultimate sense sensory impressions are not specifiable with regard to kind. Apart from Georg Friedrich Wilhelm Hegel (1807, 1812) few philosophers seem to have assumed that the particular and the universal are inseparable. In developing his dialectical system Hegel started out assuming that the particular could not be distinguished from the universal. Unfortunately he did not attempt to develop this position into an account of perception. (Brief reviews of the problems of accounting for the particular and the universal are given in A. D. Woozley, 1967; an exposition of Hegel's position is found in J. N. Findlay, 1964.) Within experimental psychology Richard Herrnstein and co-workers have questioned the position taken by the British empiristicsts to the problem of the particular and the universal. They have pointed out that their surprising findings concerning discriminatory capacities in the pidgeon are not easily reconciled with the belief that the general or universal arises as a result of learning. (For a review of this work, see Richard Herrnstein and Peter de Villiers, 1980.)

I shall begin my discussion of the problem of accounting for the relationship between the particular and the universal by an examination of how the world appears to us in perception.

The structure of perception

As made clear by Edward Boring (1948), the physicists and physiologists who established the scientific study of perception did their work within a phenomenological tradition. They were not affected by the Humboldtian idea that language structured cognition, but seem to have taken for granted that the point of departure for a scientific study of perception must be taken in descriptions of how the world appears to us. The two leading research workers Hermann von Helmholtz and Ewald Hering disagreed as to how much emphasis was to be placed on phenomenological reports, but they both believed that accurate phenomenological descriptions were essential for their study. The phenomenological orientation was strengthened by the generation of research workers studying perception at the beginning of the 20th century.

The scientists who established the scientific study of perception proceeded in a simple and straightforward manner. They assumed that characteristics inherent in the sensory impressions structured man's perceptual world. On the basis of these characteristics they classified the various sensory impressions. The most fundamental characteristics were those which determined belongingness to the diverse sensory modalities and they started out dividing the field of research into vision, audition, olfaction, gustation, proprioception and the tactile senses. Next, they differentiated impressions received through the diverse modalities according to characteristics, such as colour, shape, size, pitch, loudness, coldness, warmth, saltiness, sweetness, etc. They conceived of the latter types of characteristics as well as of movement as representing dimensions which allowed them to order impressions in a quantitative manner. The positions of objects in space were also treated as variations along dimensions.

On the basis of the classification I have outlined, the early research workers of perception proceeded to search for anatomical structures and physiological mechanisms which might explain why sensory impressions possessed the characteristics attributed to them. Like scientists of the other branches of science, the research workers studying perception have met with difficulties of classification. For example, it has proved difficult to characterize olfactory impressions. However, on the whole the straightforward belief of the pioneer scientists of perception that the characteristics they attached to sensory impressions represent an aspect of reality has proved to be highly productive. For more than one hundred years the study of perception has progressed.

On one important point the approach of the pioneer research workers was modified. Inspired by the metaphysical beliefs of the British empiricist philosophers they assumed that sensations in the form of impressions, such as colours, shapes, sizes, pitches, loudnesses, impressions of pressures and proprioception represented the ultimate constituents of all sensory impressions. In accordance with this view they tried to analyze all sensory impressions into constituents in the form of sensations. At the beginning of the 20th century a group of German psychologists reacted to this analysis of perception. They pointed out that the various parts of the perceptual field interacted with each other to produce wholes or Gestalts which were not analyzable into sensations. They drew attention to phenomena, such as those of the figure-ground relationship, the colour, shape and size constancies in the perception of material objects. This group of psychologists called Gestalt psychologists formulated a number of principles aimed at accounting for the interactions between various parts of the perceptual field. Many of these principles are controversial. However, their view of the perception of material objects has been widely accepted. Today most empirical research workers tend to agree that material objects represent wholes which cannot be regarded as combinations of sensations, such as colour, shape, size and solidity. They are perceived as entities having as their attributes sensations such as those mentioned.

According to this way of looking at the perception of material objects they represent fundamental characteristics of sensory impressions. Thus the fact that we see rocks, trees, stones, sand, snow, ice, water, houses, cars, chairs, human and animal bodies represents important characteristics of our perceptual world. These characteristics give structure to perception because they organize sensations in definite ways.

A fourth important type of perceptual structure arises from the fact that sensory impressions are registered relative to our own bodies. The sensory systems have evolved as means of regulating relationships between the organism and its environment. As a result objects are perceived as having definite relationships to our own bodies. We feel pressure on the skin of various parts of the body, locate pains in diverse parts of the body, hear sounds as coming from behind or in front of us, and see lights or material bodies to the right, or the left, up or down in our visual field. Hence, sensory impressions are organized around our own bodies.

Summing up this brief and schematic account of characteristics pertaining to sensory impressions we can say that our perceptual world is structured in the sense that impressions belong to definite sensory modalities, that impressions belonging to a specific sensory modality are further differentiated into impressions of colour, shape, size, pitch, loudness, coldness, saltiness, etc., that material objects appear as entities having various types of attributes, and that sensory impressions are registered relative to our own body. By means of the characteristics mentioned man's sensory impressions are organized into a number of specific categories.

The characteristics which I have listed seem to be fundamental in the sense that it is hardly possible to describe perception without making assumptions about them. As I pointed out in Chapter 2, knowledge from comparative anatomy and physiology as well as results of experiments of discriminatory capacities in individuals of a number of biological species strongly suggest that many of the reactions to the external world found in man are based upon mechanisms having evolved far down in man's phylogenensis. The sensory mechanisms and discriminatory capacities found in the chimpanzee are very similar to those found in man, and most likely individuals of these species perceive the world in a manner very similar to that of man. On the basis of evidence of the types mentioned, it seems to be a safe conclusion that in a fundamental sense the world of perception has the same structure for all normal, human individuals. In a fundamental sense perception is not affected by the personal experiences of an individual, of language and of the culture in which the individual grows up. This means that the structure of perception can form a common basis for the development of understanding and for the acquisition of language in human individuals.

In developing the view I have advanced on the structure of perception, I have assumed that sensory impressions have only one characteristic. On might perhaps object that sensory impressions can have more than one characteristic. Apparently, when we see a material object of some definite kind, say, a stone, we note the colour, the shape, size and position of the object. Therefore, one might hold that we see an object which has the following characteristics: the characteristic 'being a stone' and the characteristics: 'colour', 'shape', 'size' and also the attribute of having a specific location in space. I think the view of the Gestalt psychologists is a more reasonable one. They would probably have insisted that what we see is a specific material object having certain attributes and being located in a specific position. Admittedly subtle mechanisms of attention are involved which allow us to concentrate on any of the attributes as well as on the location in space. Attention can be directed in such a manner that we may perhaps primarily note what is an attribute of the stone. However, when no specific effort is made to concentrate on the attributes, what we see is a material object of the kind stone and not simultaneously a material object of the kind stone *and* a certain colour *and* a a certain shape *and* a certain location, etc. If this conclusion is correct, a group of human individuals tends to receive an impression having the same *characteristic.* Consequently if an individual points to the stone, other individuals will ordinarily understand that what is pointed to is a material object of the kind 'stone'.

Scientists are still largely ignorant of the mechanisms which operate when we perceive material objects. However, I do not think it is reasonable to believe that, say, the colours seen when we perceive material objects of definite kinds represent a subclass of the class of material objects. We cannot define material objects of definite kinds by reference to a list of attributes. As I have emphasized, the attributes are organized into a unity. This point was, as I mentioned above, overlooked by British empiricist philosophers and the early scientists studying perception.

One might perhaps think that another type of evidence against the view I have advanced is to be found in the following fact: Sensory impressions which have characteristics, such as 'colour', 'shape', and 'size', belong to the modality of vision. Consequently, they must have this characteristic in addition to the characteristic of being either a colour, a shape, or a size. Apparently what we see is either a patch of colour, a certain shape or a certain size. We do not see something which in addition to having the perceptual characteristic of being a colour, a shape or a size has the characteristic of being a visual impression. Again it seems safe to conclude that we do not at one instance have an impression which has the characteristic 'colour', 'shape', or 'size' and at another the characteristic 'visual impression'. Also on this point the perceptual world is structured in the same manner to all normal, adult human individuals.

Comment on the nature of the particular and the universal

As I hope to have made clear, it is a fundamental feature of sensory impressions that they have definite characteristics. It does not seem possible to find a situation in which a human individual perceives something which does not have a specific characteristic. A characteristic is a universal. Consequently, to say that all sensory impressions have characteristics is to say that the universal inheres in all perceptual impressions. If this line of reasoning is correct the belief that sensory impressions can be particulars in the sense that they do not have a characteristic must be rejected. Let me refer to the idea that sensory impressions can have no characteristic by the term 'pure particulars'. As I have already mentioned, the idea of pure particulars seems to be underlying the metaphysical systems of John Locke, George Berkeley, and David Hume. Actually, I think the admission of this idea into their systems was a result of their acceptance of the Cartesean dualism between body and mind. Only if we assume two different realms: A res extensa and a res cogitans, does it seem meaningful to assume the existence of 'pure particulars'. Unless the mind is ascribed the power of attributing characteristics to physical events which have no perceptual or mental characteristics, does it make sense to speak of 'pure particulars'. Hence, as I see it, there is no need to adduce *empirical* evidence against the idea of the British empiricists that ultimately perceiving is of 'pure particulars'.

The idea that perception is ultimately composed of 'pure particulars' seems to be persistent in British philosophy. At least in certain periods Bertrand Russell (1956) seems to have believed in this type of particulars and in a review article on the nature of universals Woozley (1967, p. 194) wrote:

> That in some sense or other there are universals, and that in some sense or other they are abstract objects—that is, objects of thought

> rather than of sense perception—no philosopher would wish to dispute; the difficulties begin when we try to be more precise.

If all sensory impressions have definite characteristics, the universal cannot be an object of thought as maintained by Woozley, but must somehow be inherent in perception. If we begin the examination of the problem of universals by assuming that universals are objects of thought we have already confused the issue.

When we reject the belief that perception can be of 'pure particulars' it seems to follow that it is difficult to understand what can be meant by classes having only one member. To speak of a characteristic we must at least have two members. As the reader will know, many logicians operate with classes having only one member.

On the basis of an examination of perception it seems reasonable to reject the belief that what ultimately exists are particulars in the sense of 'pure particulars'. Also, because it is difficult to understand what can be meant by a universal which is not instantiated in some way, it seems reasonable to rule out as another extreme the belief—which seems to have been the one held by Plato—that what ultimately exists are universals. It is hardly possible to conceive of a universal unless it is manifested in a particular instance. The only particulars which seem to be discernible in perception are particulars having definite characteristics, such as specific rocks, stones, trees, colours, shapes, sizes, pitches, loudnesses, human bodies. It should be noted that because hardly two instances of perception are identical *what we perceive are particulars, but they are not particulars which do not have a specific characteristic.*

In my treatment of the problem of categorizing sensory impressions I have assumed that each sensory impression has a specific characteristic and that this characteristic is the same for all members of a category. However, as we all know, characteristics may be more or less distinct and we may wonder whether an impression should be placed in the one or in the other category. For example, should an impression be classified as a tree or a bush, as a child or an adult. To take better care of this difficulty we might instead of assuming that sensory impressions have specific characteristics which are the same for all members of a category, assume that sensory impressions merely resemble each other to different degrees. This way of looking at the problem was suggested by Hume and later elaborated by Bertrand Russell and H. H. Price. (For a review of this way of looking at the nature of universals, see Woozley, ibid.)

Prima facie the two ways of looking at the problem seem to be clearly opposed to each other. However, a little reflection makes clear that it may be difficult to distinguish between them. Suppose we have rated all sensory impressions with regard to resemblance and have obtained as a result that some impressions tend to be rated as resembling certain other impressions to a high degree, but are rated as resembling all other impressions to a low degree, we may then group the impressions resembling each other to a high degree together. Whether we now should say that these impressions belong to the same category or that they have a common characteristic seems to amount to the same. The impressions we have grouped into the category are not only different from the impressions not grouped into the category, they are also similar to each other. Of course, it would probably be difficult to undertake a rating of the type suggested. One may wonder how meaningful it is to ask to what extent sensory impressions of different sensory modalities resemble each other. Apparently, impressions belonging to certain sensory modalities have features in common. For example, the senses of touch and vision both give information about the extension of objects. As the reader will know, it is possible to teach individuals born blind to orient themselves to optic stimulation when this stimulation is transformed into vibratory stimulation perceived by the sensory organs located in the skin. However, many types of comparisons across modalities would probably be extremely difficult. For example, should we say that impressions of smell and pain are more similar to impressions of, say, colour than of pitch. I think it is highly plausible to believe that if sensory impressions across modalities could be rated with regard to similarity the result would be that some impressions would have a high degree of resemblance to certain other impressions and only a low degree of resemblance to other impressions. As mentioned, this would mean that the two ways of looking at categorization might not be distinguishable from each other.

It will be noted that if sensory impressions resembled each other in such a way that they fell into clear categories it would probably be advantageous to group them into categories. This is so because it would help the organism to react more systematically to its environment. Hence, whether we say that the categorization of sensory impressions is a result of the fact that sensory impressions are identical in specific respects or that they are merely resembling each other to different degrees may be a matter of little consequence.

In Chapter 2 I mentioned the difficulty of defining perception, of distinguishing between perceiving, remembering, imagining and thinking. Actually, whether we should say that each sensory impression has a specific characteristic or merely that sensory impressions resemble each other to varying degrees, may depend upon how we define perception. I think one may argue that a defining characteristic of perception is that at any specific point an object appears with only one characteristic. If this course is taken, one might say that the fact that impressions resemble each other is a result of thinking, not of perception. One might further say that in order to speak meaningfully of resemblance one has to presuppose definite perceptual characteristics. According to this way of looking at matters it does not make sense to compare sensory impressions to each other accross sensory modalities. If this line of reasoning were to be valid, David Hume and his follower Bertrand Russell may be said to have based their arguments on a doubtful use of the word "resemblance". However, as I hope to have made clear, the problem may at present at least not be an important one.

It must be noted that if the possibility that sensory impressions merely resemble each other cannot be excluded, it does not follow that the categories into which sensory impressions are grouped are arbitrary conventions or a result of the use of language. Nor does it follow that sensory categories can have only one member. Attention should also be called to the fact that it does not make sense to define perception or information by reference only to differences in sensory impressions. To say what is meant by a perceptual task or by information, we shall have to refer to a characteristic of some sort. Hence, as done by many behaviourist psychologists, to substitute the term 'perception' for the term 'discrimination' is not warranted. (For a discussion of this point, see Saugstad, 1965.) Nor is it warranted, to conclude as done by Gregory Bateson (1979, p. 99), that "information consists of differences that make a difference".

As mentioned above, the possibility that sensory impressions are merely resembling each other and are not identical with regard to some specific characteristic cannot be excluded; because this possibility cannot be excluded, members of a category may be regarded as having to a varying extent the characteristic which determines membership in the category. In other words, members of a category may be more or less representative of the category. Instead of saying that, for example, all impressions of sound are identical with regard to the charcteristic 'sound', one might say that certain sounds are more characteristic of sounds than certain others, or instead of saying that impressions of chromatic colours are identical with regard to being chromatic colours, we might say that certain impressions of chromatic colours are more representative than others. During the last two decades psychologists have approached the empirical study of concept formation along this line of reasoning. (For a review of the original thinking underlying this approach, see Posner and Keele, 1968; Rosch, 1978.) The most representative members of a category have been termed 'prototypes'. It seems to me that if a category is clearly distinguishable from other categories, as the category 'sound', for example, appears to be from other categories representing sensory modalities, it is difficult to say that a member has more of a characteristic than another member. However, when impressions belonging to one category is not always clearly distinguishable from impressions belonging to other categories it makes more sense to speak of representativity or prototypicality. For example, impressions of chromatic colour may frequently not be clearly distinguishable from impressions of achromatic colours. In this case it seems to be meaningful to assert that, say, a well saturated green colour is more representative of chromatic colour than a diluted green colour. The category bird has been used as another example. Certain species of bird, such as the ostrich and the penguin, appear as less representative of the category 'bird' than, say, robins. Apparently, the problem of deciding what can be meant by a prototype is an intricate one. Fortunately for my purposes, it does not seem to matter whether I regard members belonging to a category as identical or merely resembling each other with regard to the characteristic determining membership in the category, and I shall leave the problem here. However, in the next chapter I shall comment upon the Wittgensteinian idea of 'family resemblance' which seems to have been an inspiration to the approach to the study of concept formation mentioned above.

The structure of knowledge

The examination of perception undertaken in this chapter has revealed that all our sensory impressions seem to posess definite characteristics, that they are members of definite categories. What I referred to as 'pure particulars' does not seem to be present in perception. I think it is natural to believe that this fundamental feature of perception is maintained in all types of knowledge which man can acquire. According to this way of looking at matters, the unique instance, i.e. an instance which is conceived of as not possessing any characteristics, is a an abstraction. As I pointed out in the beginning of the present chapter, it represents no argument for the unique instance, the 'pure particular', that we are able to attribute a number of characteristics to the various types of material bodies. For example, we may attribute the following characteristics to a particular stone: 'colour', 'shape', 'size', 'solidity', 'roughness', 'moveableness', 'being a stone', etc. The very fact that we are able to attribute a number of characteristics to the stone does not mean that we are able to perceive or specify "something" in this object which is not the member of a category. The same is, of course, true of human individuals. We are able to attribute a large number of characteristics to them, but we are not able to perceive or to specify something which is not the member of a category. The idea of a pure particular, of the unique instance, in the sense discussed here, thus represents an abstraction. In line with this reasoning it is plausible to believe that the things we remember, imagine and think of are members of definite categories.

Instead of believing that knowledge of an abstract type has a structure which is entirely different from the one found in perception, it seems more natural to assume that abstract knowledge represents an elaboration of information or knowledge received through sensory perception. I shall indicate what appear as fairly obvious elaborations of the structure inherent in perception. As I pointed out, in a large variety of situations we tend to perceive material objects having attributes, such as colour, shape, size and solidity. Since attention is focussed on material objects, specific spatial relationships between them may be noted. Objects are perceived as being over and under each other, inside each other, to the right or to the left of each other. In this way categories denoting spatial relationships between material objects may arise. Furthermore, because attention is focussed on the material objects, movements are naturally ascribed to them and in this way categories containing instances of various types of movements, such as 'fast', 'slow', 'rhythmical' and 'jerky', may arise.

A fundamental feature of the way the world appears to us is that material objects are of different kinds. The categorization of material objects into different kinds is the result of learning that the diverse attributes of material objects can appear together in specific ways. Because we may discriminate between objects on the basis of a large variety of perceptual characteristics, the learning involved in this type of categorization must in many instances be of a very complicated nature. For example, plants and animals belonging to the same species may differ with regard to a number of characteristics, and the understanding that certain characteristics differentiate one species from other species, involves a number of judgements and inferences of various sorts. Think of the similarities in the appearance of cats and tigers and oranges and lemons. If we did not have a rather extensive knowledge of cats and tigers we might perhaps believe that cats were the young of tigers and similarly, if we had no knowledge of orange and lemon trees we might believe that lemons were a kind of oranges or vice versa. As we all know, until more detailed knowledge was obtained about whales they were classified as fish. For my purposes I need not go into the intricate question of how we are capable of categorizing material objects into different kinds. The only thing I wish to note is that this categorization is probably most naturally regarded as an elaboration of the fact that material objects occupy a central position in our perceptual world. Hence, even if complicated types of learning are involved in the way we categorize material objects into kinds, the categorization has an obvious basis in the structure inherent in perception. I am not arguing that this type of categorization is a result of perception alone.

Among the material bodies the human body occupies a central position. A number of characteristics allow us to categorize parts of the body, such as head, trunk, arms, legs, etc. These parts of the body are further differentiated in a number of ways. For example, the face is attributed characteristics, such as 'eyes', 'nose', mouth', 'forehead', 'chin', 'cheeks', etc. By concentrating upon the human body we are thus capable of organizing a wealth of knowledge. The categories containing this knowledge are obviously not related to each other in an arbitrary manner, but represent a definite organization.

Just as we attribute movements to inanimate bodies we attribute movements of various types to the human body. Categories of movements, such as 'walking', 'running', 'climbing', 'swimming', etc. may consequently be regarded as related to the category 'human body'. The same may be said of categories, such as 'standing', 'sitting', 'lying'. They are postures which the human body may take. Still further, expressions of emotions, such as anger, fear, joy, submission, sorrow, may be regarded as characteristics pertaining to the human body.

It does not require much imagination to understand that there may be a relatively short step from understanding that the human body may engage in movements, such as walking, running and climbing, to the understanding that it may engage in activities, such as hunting, fishing, playing. Hence, also activities, such as the latter ones may be regarded as categories organized around the human body.

The construction of a coherent and consistent theory of human knowledge is a task which will require the work of generations of scientists. The examination I have undertaken has aimed at demonstrating that human knowledge is so organized that it is possible to understand that an essential part of it is shared by all normal, adult, human individuals. I have pointed to the following features of this organization: 1. all knowledge forms part of specific categories. This means that when we perceive, remember, imagine, or think of something this something forms part of some specific category, 2. some of the categories into which human knowledge is organized are fundamental in the sense that it is not possible to account for knowledge without somehow assuming these categories, and 3. a number of categories may be regarded as elaborations of fundamental categories. This means that when the latter categories have been acquired, it is highly probable that the former ones will also be acquired.

I shall formulate the following two principles: 1. *Human knowledge is organized into categories* and 2. *some of these categories must be regarded as fundamental in the sense that it is not possible to account for knowledge without assuming their existence.*

The acquisistion of knowledge requires familiarity with the environment. Differences in the physical as well as the cultural environment create differences in the familiarity human individuals have with a variety of phenomena. As a result of these differences human individuals form different categories, acquire different types of knowledge. Furthermore, the formation of a number of categories requires reflection and understanding. The inclination to reflect upon the phenomena met with and the capacity for understanding varies from indivldual to individual and represents another source of variation in knowledge. As I see it, the belief that human individuals have extensive parts of their knowledge in common, is not in opposition to the fact that there are differences in knowledge among them. As I hope to make clear in Chapter 7, use of language has a basis not only in the fact that human individuals have a common knowledge, but also in the fact that there are differences in the knowledge they possess. In the attempts made at accounting for language this latter fact seems to have been overlooked by scientists and philosophers. In Chapter 7 I shall discuss differences in knowledge among human individuals. I shall show that information as transmitted by language must be defined with regard to these differences.

On the nature of concepts

Earlier in the present chapter I mentioned that attempts at accounting for the relationship between concepts raise a problem which I do not think has a definite solution. Instead of trying to solve this problem, I shall show that it is possible to give an adequate account of language without first having to solve it. The problem I have in mind is the following. Our understanding of a concept, such as 'tree' is dependendent upon an understanding of other concepts, say, such as 'leaf', 'branch', 'trunk', and 'root'. If our understanding of all concepts depended upon an understanding of other concepts it is difficult to see how our understanding of concepts can have a definite basis. On the other hand, if our understanding of concepts is based upon an understanding of one or more concepts which are not dependent upon other concepts, it is difficult to imagine what can be meant by concepts of this type. An individual who possessed only one single concept would not be able to distinguish between the members of the category and the concept. Hence, the idea of a concept would lose its meaning. It will be understood that it is no solution to the problem to assume, as some logicians do, that there are categories or classes which have one member only.

If it is correct to say that concepts can only be defined relative to each other, it seems to follow that we cannot give an adequate account of the nature of concepts. Apparently, when such an account cannot be given, it is difficult to state clearly what can be meant by the extension and intension of a class or category. The distinction between the extension and intension of a class or category is based upon the assumption that a distinction can be drawn between the members contained in the class or catgeory and the concept determining membership in the category. If we cannot say what is meant by a concept it is difficult to understand on what basis this distinction can be drawn. Actually, modern logicians, such as Saul Kripke (1972) and Hillary Putnam (1975) have argued forcefully against the possibility of drawing this distinction. (It must be noted that they are linguistic philosophers and speak of 'terms' where I speak of 'concepts'.)

As made clear by Putnam (ibid), if it is not possible to draw a clear line of division between the extension and the intension of a class or category it is not possible to give an adequate account of concepts or of classes or categories in terms of components. (For reviews of treating words as consisting of components, see Clark and Clark, 1976; Lyons, 1977.) Also, it must be understood that it is problematic to account for categories in terms of prototypes, as suggested by Rosch (ibid). As made clear by Stephen Schwartz (1977), the Wittgensteinian suggestion that concepts can be treated as clusters of properties also becomes dubious when it is realized that it is hardly possible to draw a clear line of division between the intension and extension of a class or category or, as the linguistic philosopher would express matters, between the extension and intension of a *term*.

Because we cannot state in an adequate manner what is meant by a concept, one might be tempted to draw the conclusion that concepts are fictitious entities. In their attack upon the belief that words have meaning and are the names of concepts, Austin (1961) and Gilbert Ryle (1948, 1957) seem to have succumbed to this temptation. Whatever status one attributes to concepts it is a fact that experience or knowledge is ordered into categories. As I have emphasized, we see trees, rocks, animal bodies, etc. and not something which does not belong to any category. As I argued in Chapter 3, it is implausible to believe, as evidently done by Austin and Oxford philosophers, that the categories into which knowledge is organized, are the result merely of man's use of language. I think we shall have to regard it as a fact that human individuals perceive and conceive of objects in the form of members of definite categories and not in the form of what I have referred to as 'pure particulars'. Apparently, from the fact that we cannot give a satisfactory definition of the term 'concept', it does not follow that concepts are fictitious entities.

For the scientific study of cognition it may represent a serious obstacle to progress that so little is known about concepts, about the characteristics which determine membership in categories. However, even if the scientific study of language is dependent upon the study of cognition, this ignorance need not be so serious. This is so because, irrespective of culture and specific training, all human individuals who have undergone a normal intellectual development have an understanding of a large variety of concepts. If language, as I see it, is regarded as a means of making reference to these concepts, to understand the use of language the point of departure can be taken in the understanding the ordinary speaker has of concepts, such as those I have discussed earlier in this chapter. Serious difficulties only arise when—like linguists and analytic philosophers—

one believes that perception and thinking cannot be distinguished from language and its use. In the next chapter I shall show how language can have a basis in concepts of the types discussed in the present chapter, and in Chapter 7 I shall show that linguistic signs defined by reference to concepts can have the functions ascribed to language.

Chapter 6

The structure of language

This in turn makes word meanings anything but arbitrary. They are constrained to follow the classifications of experience by the human conceptual apparatus, which is there independent of language. This view of word meaning has several important implications. First, the categories that are named in a language should depend on the way its users conceive of the world. Second, children should build their first attempts in using words on the conceptual components already available to them. And third, these components should be apparent in all languages.

Herbert Clark and Eve Clark. *Psychology and Language*, p. 442.

In Chapter 4 I suggested that knowledge about language might be integrated by conceiving of it as an assembly of instruments for the transmittance of information. To make this idea useful to empirical research it is necessary to find a way which makes it possible to describe its form or structure as well as its use according to this idea.

To arrive at a conception of language as an assembly of instruments I shall take the point of departure in the belief that in some way speaking is a manipulation of words. Introspective reports suggest that the speaker operates upon words to produce utterances in the form of sentences. This way of looking at matters points in the direction that words are the instruments for communication. The sentence is the product of the operation and is thus not an instrument. Introspective reports of what the speaker is doing can, of course, only provide a hint for our search regarding the instrument. To demonstrate that the word and not the sentence is the instrument we shall have to construct a model based upon this belief, and then find ways of evaluating the adequacy of the model. Accordingly, I shall begin by assuming that words are instruments for the transmittance of information.

To function as instruments for the transmittance of information words must possess meaning. Apparently, if contrary to my belief word meaning should be dependent upon the use made of sentences, it is difficult to imagine what is the structure and use of words. Therefore, to construct a useful model on the idea that words are instruments, one must show that words obtain their meaning independently of the use made of them in sentences. They must have a form or a structure which allows us to conceive of them independently of their use in utterances in the form of sentences. Actually, in the history of the study of language many thinkers have believed that words obtain their meaning from a reference to knowledge of an extra-linguistic nature. In the 20th century this belief was discredited by linguists and analytic philosophers. As I made clear in Chapter 3, linguists and analytic philosophers have not been willing to accept that thinking and language are different things and that most likely language has a basis in thinking. Also, they do not seem to have been willing to accept that man's perception and thinking may have a structure which can form the basis for the determination of the meaning of words. True enough, they have pointed to a number of difficulties met with in attempts at explaining word meaning in this manner. However, in making this criticism they have overlooked that the information an individual obtains from a verbal utterance need not arise only from the meaning of the words contained in the utterance. The information transmitted only partly arises from the meaning of the words. *Information is a result also of the interpretation of the utterance by the listener, and the listener is in the possession of a number of extra-linguistic cues for the interpretation of the utterance.* When this apparently simple and straightforward view is accepted, it is easy to see that many of the arguments raised against the old belief as to how word meaning arises lose their force. In the next chapter I shall discuss how the listener interprets the utterance by means of cues of an extra-linguistic nature. In the present chapter I shall point to the fact that there seems to be a correspondence between the structure of man's knowledge and the meaning of a variety of different types of words.

How words derive their meanings

In Chapter 1 I pointed out that not all morphemes are of equal importance for verbal communication. This point is essential to understand not only how language can have its functions, but also to understand what its structure is.

Words, I shall hold, are signs which are made up of phonemes and which are defined by means of definite referents. I shall regard all types of words as names and shall divide names into two main types: 1. common names and 2. proper names. A 'common name', I shall say, is defined by its reference to the characteristic, the concept, which determines membership in a certain category. For example, the common name 'tree' in the

English language is defined by its reference to the concept 'tree' and the common name 'colour' is defined by its reference to the concept 'colour'. It must be noted that it is the common name and not the concept which is defined. To understand the definition of a common name one must be able to *identify* the concept, but *it is not necessary to be able to define the concept*. The problem of defining concepts I discussed in the previous chapter. The common name denotes that something is a member (members) of a certain category. It does not denote a specific member (specific members). A proper name refers to a specific, particular member of a category. Because it refers to a member of a category, I think it must be ascribed meaning and I shall say that it is defined by its reference. For example, the proper name 'Mary' is defined by its reference to a specific individual of the category 'female, human individual' and the proper name 'Africa' to a specific member of the category 'geographical parts of the world'. It will be noted that according to the present conception of how common and proper names are defined, the two types of names are similar and the use of the term 'common name' seems to be appropriate.

Below I shall show that it is plausible to believe that a number of different types of common and proper names obtain their meaning in the way I have indicated above. Because this belief is opposed to dominant beliefs concerning word meaning current in Western linguistics and philosophy, it is important to show that it can be made plausible. Due to the fact that no acceptable scientific theory of cognition is available it is at present not possible to give a more rigorous demonstration that the belief is correct. I shall follow the procedure I outlined in Chapter 4 and try to show that the beliefs upon which I shall rest my theoretical model are plausible.

Common names

In the previous chapter I pointed to a number of characteristics which contribute to the structure of perception. These characteristics are of such a nature that it is easy to see that a large number of linguistic signs may be defined with reference to them. I shall here repeat the main points I made concerning the structure of man's perception. In the first place, perception is structured into categories in the form of modalities. The characteristics determining membership in these categories make possible the definition of sensory verbs, such as the English: *see*, *hear*, *smell*, *taste*, *feel*. Secondly, the impressions received through the diverse sensory modalities are differentiated by characteristics such as 'colour', 'shape', 'size', 'loudness', 'pitch', 'sweetness', 'saltiness', 'coldness', 'warmth'. Some characteristics are further differentiated. For example, impressions of colour are differentiated by characteristics, such as 'white', 'grey', 'black', 'red', 'green', impressions of shape by characteristics such as 'square', 'round', 'triangular', and impressions of size by characteristics, such as 'large' and 'small'. Characteristics, such as those mentioned, may be regarded as forming the basis for the definition of a large number of common names. A third type of characteristics arises from the fact that what is perceived is related to the body of the perceiver. Thus, we see light and material objects as located to the right, left, up or down in the visual field, and as being proximal or distal, hear sounds arising from behind or in front, feel pressures, pains, cold and warmth on specific parts of the body. Relationships of the type sensory impressions have to our body may be regarded as characteristics of perception which can form the basis for the definition of a third large group of common names.

In the previous chapter I also made clear that a number of characteristics might be regarded as elaborations of some of the perceptual characteristics which I assumed were fundamental in the sense that it is not possible to account for perception without assuming them. Characteristics of this type are movements of material objects which may be characterized as being 'fast', 'slow', 'rhythmical', 'jerky', etc. Other characteristics of this type are spatial relationships existing between objects. For example, objects are perceived as located 'over', 'under', 'to the side' of another object. This type of characteristics gives rise to the definition of still another group of linguistic signs. Some research workers might perhaps prefer to regard movements of objects and spatial relationships as directly perceived and not as elaborations of perceptual characteristics. For my purposes it does not matter whether one views it the one or the other way. The important point is that it is natural to believe that characteristics of the type mentioned here can provide the basis for the definition of a large variety of common names.

Another large group of characteristics, which I suggested could be seen as elaborations of fundamental categories, are the characteristics determining membership in categories of a natural kind, i.e., 'rock', 'stone', 'tree', 'house', 'table', 'car', 'boat', 'water', 'ice', 'cat', rat', 'horse', 'tiger', etc. Among the natural kind material objects representing food naturally occupy a central position. Just as was the case for the two groups of characteristics mentioned above, some research workers might probably insist that characteristics determining membership in categories of a natural kind are directly perceived. For my purposes it does not matter whether the one or the other way of looking at the problem is chosen.

Among the material objects the human body occupies a central position and I mentioned a number of characteristics relating to different parts of the body. I think it is easy to imagine that parts of the body, such as the head, the arms, the legs, the trunk, the face, the eyes, the nose, etc. may provide the basis for the definition of common names, such as the English words: *head*, *arm*, *trunk*, etc. Further, as I made clear in the previous chapter, just as we attribute movements to material objects, we attribute movements of various kinds to the human body. This results in characteristics, such as 'eating', 'walking', 'running', 'climbing', 'swimming'. Closely related to the movements performed by the human body are the various postures it can take, which give characteristics such as 'standing', 'sitting', 'lying'. Still further, as I suggested, expressions of emotions, such as 'anger', 'joy', 'fear', 'sorrow', 'submission', may be regarded as characteristics pertaining to the human body. The movements and postures which are registered with regard to the human body may be said to form a basis for the definition of a large variety of common names.

In connection with the movements and postures which can be registered with regard to the human body I mentioned that it was probably not a great step from understanding that there are such categories as 'walking', 'running', and 'climbing' to the understanding that there are categories such as 'playing', 'fishing', 'hunting', and 'picking berries'.

The characteristics I have listed above suggest that it is not difficult to understand that the common knowledge which human individuals have may form the basis for the definition of a considerable number of words. Furthermore, when the list is more closely examined it is noted that the words which can be defined by reference to the characteristics are of a variety of types.

Proper names

Language has a variety of different types of proper names. They are used to denote human individuals, domesticated animals, boats, geographical places, historical dates, planets, diseases, specific types of events in scientific descriptions, etc. Hence, they play a great role in language. As I mentioned earlier in this chapter, I shall assume that proper names have as referents specific members of specific categories. While we may attach proper names to specific members of a variety of different categories, there are members of some categories which we apparently do not name in this manner. For example, we do not name a specific colour or a specific tone by attaching a proper name to it. We name only members or instances which are unique, i.e. members or instances of which we can assume that there is only the one member or instance. Apparently we do not make this assumption with regard to colours or tones. As I see it, this assumption concerning uniqueness can only be made when the specific member or instance can be attributed so many characteristics that we can have a reasonable certainty that there can be only one instance denoted by the proper name. For example, members of the category human individuals can be attributed so many characteristics in addition to the characteristic of being a human individual, that we can feel certain that we have denoted a specific individual.

In the previous chapter I took the position that it is not possible to conceive of anything unless it is a member of a category. In line with this position I shall have to state that proper names have meaning or sense. As John Searle (1967) pointed out, we use different types of proper names for girls and boys, for human individuals and animals, for animals and boats, etc. This suggests that proper names are not without meaning or sense. On the other hand, the fact that proper names seem to denote instances which appear as unique, suggests that they have no meaning or sense, and consequently, contrary to what *I* have assumed, do *not* refer to a specific member of a category, but to the unique instance. The question whether or not proper names should be ascribed a sense has been hotly debated by philosophers. John Stuart Mill (1843) thought they should not be ascribed sense, while Frege (1892), believed they should be ascribed sense. More recently Saul Kripke (1972) has presented an ingenious argumentation for the position that proper names do not have a sense or meaning. For the model I am developing it is hardly a matter of great importance in what way the question is answered, but when the epistemological position I have advocated is taken it seems most reasonable to ascribe sense to proper names.

Conclusion

As I have shown, it is possible to point to facts of an extra-linguistic nature which may serve as the basis for the definition of the meaning of words of a number of different types. Words were divided into common and proper names and I shall formulate as two principles for determining word meaning what I said about common and proper names earlier in the present chapter: 1. *Common names derive their meaning from a reference to the characteristics, the concepts, which determine membership in definite categories and* 2. *proper names derive their meaning from a reference to a specific, a particular member of definite categories.* By means of these two principles and the two principles presented in the previous chapter, I shall suggest that it is possible to account for the meaning of all types of words. To avoid unnecessary misunderstandings *I want the reader to note that my position does not imply that words can be ostensively defined.*

Objections to the belief that words are names

As I mentioned earlier in this chapter, linguists and linguistic philosophers of the 20th century have raised a number of objections against the belief that words can be regarded as the names of concepts. Many of the objections raised seem to have originated in Wittgenstein's later thinking about language. I shall discuss some of the major objections.

In some of the earlier sections of *Philosophical Investigations* Wittgenstein drew attention to the fact that words have diverse uses. In section 11 he warned that the uniform appearance words have when spoken and when met in script may lead one to assume a uniformity also in their use. In section 10 he even stated that the uses of words were absolutely unlike. I shall not attempt to interpret Wittgenstein on this point, but shall just point to the following. When we look at language as a means of communication, words may seem to have in common the fact that they are used for transmittance of information. Moreover, if it is correct, as I have argued in the present chapter, that common names derive their meaning from references to characteristics or concepts determining membership in categories, they have this essential feature in common. Whether this is a sufficient means for establishing a science of semantics is a question primarily for empirical science and for the philosophy of science, and not for epistemology or logic.

A second objection against the belief that words are the names of things runs along the following lines. It is not so difficult to imagine that concrete nouns, such as *rock*, *tree*, and *house*, have a referent, but what about the more abstract types of words? In the first place, as I made clear earlier in the present chapter, it is not difficult to suggest a possible basis for the definition of a number of types of words. Secondly, it should be noted that the fact that it is difficult to account for the meaning of certain types of highly abstract words does not show that this cannot be done. This objection cannot be regarded as serious until it is shown that an alternative way of accounting for word meaning is more plausible. To my knowledge no one has made this attempt.

A *suggestion* for an alternative was possibly made by Wittgenstein (ibid, sec. 421) when he stated that one might look at the sentence as an instrument, and at its sense as its employment. Actually, as pointed out by Saussure, a consideration of the form of sentences makes it hardly more reasonable to regard *them* as the instruments rather than regarding words as the instruments, and what is more important: how could one possibly decide what the employment of sentences means unless one assumed that the words of the sentence had a meaning? It seems rather improbable that Wittgenstein should have meant that the meaning of words might be determined *solely* by the use made of sentences. What he probably meant was that it is not possible to account for the sense of a sentence unless also its use is taken into account. If this was his position it is in agreement with mine. As I indicated in Chapter 1, one must distinguish between the meaning of words and the information transmitted by the sentence containing the words. The information transmitted is a result of: 1. the meaning of the words and 2. the interpretation of the sentence by the listener. As I shall show in the next chapter, information is a result of the meaning of words and of the relationship between the speaker and the listener. According to this way of interpreting Wittgenstein he may be said to speak of the 'employment of a sentence' whereas I speak of the 'information transmitted by a sentence'. I hope to show that my way of looking at matters has certain advantages relative to that of Wittgenstein's.

Before I leave the problem of accounting for the meaning of abstract types of words I shall comment upon a frequently made complaint that nothing is gained by basing a scientific study of semantics on the notion of concepts. Lyons (1981, p. 137) stated the point in the following manner:

> In fact, there is no evidence to suggest that concepts, in any clearly defined sense of the term 'concept', are relevant to the construction of an empirically justifiable theory of linguistic semantics. Obviously nothing is gained by using the very vagueness of the term 'concept', as it is ordinarily interpreted, to protect a theory of semantics that is based upon it from refutation. We shall make no appeal to concepts in our discussion of meaning.

I think Lyons has overlooked two important points. In the first place, as I have emphasized, the term 'concept' is not as vague as the Oxford philosophers have argued that it is. Secondly, and this is, of course, central for an understanding of the nature of semantics—if we accept that thinking and language are different things and further that language has a basis in perception and thinking, it is natural to believe that word-meaning has a basis in concepts. If my assumptions concerning the relationship between thinking and language are tenable, to make the study of semantics a productive one, scientists cannot, as has been done by Lyons (1968, 1977, 1981) and most modern linguists, take their point of departure in beliefs concerning the structure of language. The point of departure must be taken from conceptions of the nature of man's perception and thinking.

A third objection against the belief that words are the names of concepts is that it is possible to refer to the same object by different words or expressions. To take Frege's classic example, we can refer to the same planet by the two expressions: *the morning star* and *the evening star* This is an objection only if we assume that no distinction can be made between the conditions under which a name is defined and the conditions under which the name is used for communication. When, as I have argued, a distinction must be drawn between, on the one hand, perception and thinking and, on the other, use of language, a distinction can be made between the two types of conditions. For example, the words: *Fido, dog*, and *animal* may be defined under one set of conditions and used under another set of conditions. I may refer to a particular dog by all three names. Hence, from the fact that the expressions: *the morning star* and *the evening star* refer to the same planet, it does not follow that the two expressions must have the same meaning.

A fourth objection is that frequently the same word has more than one meaning, so-called polysemy. Lyons (ibid) gives as an example of polysemy the word *neck* in English, which may mean: part of the body, part of a shirt or other garment, part of a bottle, or a narrow strip of land. If we assume that understanding and language are different things, it is not difficult to see that the same sign may acquire different meanings, particularly if these meanings develop successively, as they probably tend to do. Also, when we draw the distinction between understanding and language, it is not difficult to understand that a word may be used in a metaphorical sense.

Wittgenstein's (ibid) attack on the belief that words denoting sensations derive their meaning from referring to sensory impressions is famous. He argued that this belief leads to the untenable position that an individual can have a language which it is not possible for other individuals to understand, the so-called private language thesis. Peter Strawson (1966) and Fodor (ibid) have argued convincingly against this position. As I see it, Wittgenstein's argument loses its force when account is taken of the fact that in order to determine a concept, it must be related to other concepts. For example, the concept 'pain'—which was taken as the main example by Wittgenstein—is related to concepts such as 'human body', 'skin', 'wound', 'bleeding' and concepts determining parts of the human body, such as 'arm', 'leg', 'head'. If we assume that an individual has the concept 'human body' it is not difficult to imagine that pain is ascribed to the human body and hence that this sensation is shared by all human individuals. Pain is something which I can have because I have a body and also something which other individuals can have because they also have bodies. According to this way of looking at the referent for the word *pain* it is not a private experience, i.e. an experience which an individual cannot share with other individuals.

When we consider the fact that we do not only perceive the bodies of other individuals, but also parts of our own body it is not difficult to understand that we form the category 'human body' which includes the bodies of other individuals as well as our own body. To the human body pertains a skin and this skin can be wounded and bleeding may arise. This may happen to oneself as well as to other individuals. Because it is a characteristic of the body that such wounds result in impressions of pain,

pain pertains to the human body and is not a private experience in the sense that one has no basis for believing that other individuals can have the same experience. If an individual can understand that other individuals can have pain as a result of the fact that the skin has been damaged, it is not so difficult to imagine that this individual could also have the understanding that other individuals could have pain in an interior part of the body. In discussing this problem one must take care that one does not set as a requirement to knowledge that it must be absolutely certain. No knowledge is absolutely certain. One must suggest a plausible account. As I see it, such an account is obtainable when the point of departure is taken from the fact that concepts are related to each other in a number of ways. It does not make sense to treat concepts as if they existed independently of each other. It should be noted that *in my treatment of concepts I have not assumed that they are mental images attainable by introspection.*

The structure of language

In the previous chapter I argued that knowledge is organized independently of language and in the present chapter I have shown that it is possible to explain the meaning of a large variety of different types of words by assuming that they are defined by reference to the way knowledge is organized. Thus I think it is highly plausible to believe that word-meaning is established by reference to facts of an extra-linguistic nature. This conclusion runs counter to the central belief of 20th century linguistics that language is a system composed of elements whose meaning is determined by their relationships to each other. Hence, I think the central idea of modern linguistics must be rejected. Instead of conceiving of language as a system of signs, I shall conceive of it as an assembly of words which derive their meaning from references to facts of an extra-linguistic nature, and which act as instruments of communication.

In Chapter 1 I underlined that the idea that language is a system has proved useful in the study of the elementary sounds making up the linguistic signs. I shall say that the words—and in general the morphemes—are structured in such a way that they are composed of phonemes according to the phonological rules of the diverse languages. Thus words—and in general morphemes—can be said to have a definite structure.

There are many types of words. However, this fact need not preclude that it can be useful to regard them as instruments. If words can be shown to have the same function, one may still regard them as the same kind of instrument even if their form varies. I shall suggest that in analogy with the use our ancestors made of stones, words can be conceived of as instruments. A number of different types of stones might be used as a weapon to be thrown after a prey or an ememy. Even if the size and shape of the stones may vary, onc can still rcgard the stones thrown as weapons, as the same instrument. Also, even if stones were refined to be more appropriate for being thrown, one can speak of them as the same kind of instruments. Hence, the fact that there are a number of different types of words need not prevent one from regarding them as instruments.

In order that the analogy between words and instruments shall be a useful one, it must be possible to ascribe a meaning to words which is more or less invariant from utterance to utterance. By assuming that words derive their meaning from a fixed referent, it is possible to ascribe a meaning to them which does not vary from utterance to utterance. However, if words are ascribed a fixed meaning the problem arises that it is possible to use the same word (or the same words) to transmit different types of information. To this problem I shall turn in the next chapter. Before I try to explain how it is possible to communicate with words which have a more or less fixed meaning, I shall make an observation on what I believe to be a characteristic of the vocabulary.

Apparently the vocabularies of speech communities undergo more or less continuous changes in the way that new words are included and old ones drop out. The vocabulary of the individual speaker increases rapidly in the period of childhood in which the individual acquires language. When speakers have reached adulthood their vocabularies do not undergo such rapid changes as they did in childhood. However, they are still able to learn to use new words with great ease. So, while it may be difficult to explain how an individual acquires her or his first words, *it hardly represents a great problem to explain how a vocabulary consisting of a limited number of words can be extended.* This means that, if it can be explained how it is possible to communicate by means of a restricted number of words, it hardly represents a great problem to explain how the number of words can be extended. In line with this way of reasoning I shall concentrate my account on how it can be explained that communication can be carried out by means of a limited number of words.

Chapter 7

Use of language

Our own theory distinguishes between the meaning of an expression and its interpretation in a particular utterance.

Jon Barwise and John Perry, *Situations and Attitudes*, pp. 31-32, 1983.

In Chapters 5 and 6 I have accounted for the form, the structure, of language. In the present chapter I shall give an account of how I believe language is used for communication. In describing the linguistic instrument a main problem was to explain how words can have a basis in a knowledge shared by the speakers of a language. No account of language can be regarded as satisfactory unless it explains how language can be a public property. However, to understand the use made of language, attention must be shifted to differences in knowledge between the individuals speaking a language. *Language has a basis in a common knowledge, but also in a difference in knowledge between individuals.* In the present chapter I shall turn to the problem of explaining how words which have a basis in a common knowledge can be used to overcome differences in knowledge between the speaker and the listener.

Individuals using an instrument perform or behave in certain ways. This means that in order to describe the use of language I shall have to describe a certain type of behaviour. In Chapters 2 and 3 I pointed out that little work had been devoted to problems met with in attempts at describing use of language. As a result, in their treatments of linguistic problems, empirical research workers as well as philosophers seem to have overlooked seemingly obvious points.

The goals of the speaker and the listener

To describe behaviour in an adequate manner one must, as emphasized by Tolman (1932), begin by making clear what is the goal of the organism exhibiting the behaviour. Apparently, verbal communication is a form of social interaction and, as I mentioned in Chapter 2, Mead contributed to an understanding of this specific type of interaction by calling attention to the fact that consciousness and the capacity for using language had been developed by individuals learning to take the role of other individuals in interacting with one another. H. P. Grice (1967) shed light on speech acts by developing the idea that in verbal communication the speaker and the listener must cooperate. He suggested various principles which seem to govern this cooperation. More recently Clark and Clark (1976, p. 25) have made clear that in producing their utterances speakers must take into consideration what is on the minds of their listeners:

> First, speakers intend to have some effect on their listeners, and must get them to recognize these intentions. The sentences used must therefore reflect these intentions. Second, speakers want to convey certain ideas and to do this the sentences must also reflect the listeners' ways of thinking about objects, states, events, and facts. And third, speakers must have some conception of what is on their listeners' minds at the moment and of where they want the communication to lead. The sentences used must reflect these conceptions as well.

Clark and Clark rightly emphasized that speakers must do something relative to their listeners, but what about the listeners: are they merely passive receivers of information or must they also do something to receive the information? Few research workers seem to have gone into this question.

It does not take much reflection to understand that unless listeners are doing something, performing in certain ways, they shall not receive information from verbal utterances. Even simple descriptions or assertions such as can be achieved by an utterance such as "The door is open", presupposes that the listener has a knowledge of the situation in which it is produced as well as a knowledge of the individual uttering it. The listener might, for example, not know that there was a door, or she or he might believe that the speaker was lying. Evidently, to receive information from verbal utterances listeners must make a number of correct judgements, and to be able to make these they must have certain types of knowledge. It does not seem possible to imagine any type of utterance which can be understood without the active participation of the listener.

Because transmittance of information ultimately depends upon the activities of the listener, *speakers* have no means of producing their utterances so that they can have a guarantee that they will be understood. It must be noted that this is so whether speakers make their utterances in the form of single words, phrases, or in the form of sentences. No magic inheres in the sentence.

I shall consider a little more closely the relationship between the speaker and the listener. An obvious requirement of individuals who are to transmit information, is that they possess the knowledge of what they are to transmit. An equally obvious requirement for individuals who are to receive some information or knowledge, is that they do not already possess this knowledge. This means that in order to be able to transmit information the speaker must possess some knowledge which the listener does not have. Another way of expressing this simple fact is to say that *verbal communication centres around differences in knowledge between the individuals participating in it.* I think it is highly plausible to believe that the behaviour of speakers and listeners is guided by this fact and shall use it to formulate the goal of the speaker and the listener (my fifth postulate): *In verbal communication the goal of the speaker is to adjust the knowledge of another individual (the listener) to be identical in some definite respect to her/his own knowledge and the goal of the listener is to have her/his knowledge adjusted to be identical in some definite respect to that of the speaker.*

When one considers that in the course of their ontogenetic development human individuals establish a large variety of relationships to each other, it will be understood that an individual enters the dialogue with considerable knowledge about the other individual participating in the dialogue. On the basis of this knowledge the speaker has an understanding of what may represent information to the listener and the listener has an understanding of what the speaker is going to say. In other words, both the speaker and the listener are in possession of a number of cues which guide their conversation. The point I am making is that on the basis of such cues the listener is capable of transforming the meaning of the words contained in an utterance into information. According to this way of looking at matters, it is not possible to infer from a verbal utterance the information transmitted by it, unless account is taken of the relationship between the speaker and the listener.

More recently, Barwise and Perry (1983) broke away from the Frege-tradition in semantics and approached problems along the lines I have drawn above and which I (Saugstad, 1980) had drawn a couple of years prior to the appearance of their stimulating book. In agreement with their position I can say that also my "theory distinguishes between the meaning of an expression and its interpretation in particular utterances".

Before I turn to the problem of describing the performance of the speaker and the listener I shall discuss an important point which concerns the use of the term 'knowledge' or 'information'.

Knowledge may be more or less available

In Chapter 2 I made clear that at present psychologists are unable to describe stimuli by reference to physical dimensions. Clearly, if stimuli cannot be so described, it is not possible to describe the information transmitted in verbal communication in physicalist terms. If this had been possible, we should have a much better foundation for the study of the use of language. But this is a distant goal and at present we shall have to use the term 'information' more or less in accordance with everyday use of language. As I mentioned in Chapters 1 and 2, psychologists in the information processing tradition use the terms 'information' and 'knowledge' as synonyms. Also, the use of the terms is not restricted to knowledge acquired only through study, but is extended to include events which are perceived, remembered, imagined and thought of. I shall use the terms in this extended manner. However, I want to call attention to an important point in the treatment of problems concerning human knowledge which I think is frequently overlooked.

The point I have in mind is that when one attributes knowledge of some kind to some individuals, one does this on the basis of their performance in certain types of situations and at a certain time. But, as we all know, knowledge which we possess at some definite time may not be available at other times. Also, knowledge which may be available in *certain types* of situations may not be available when the situation is changed. We are all familiar with the difficulty of identifying persons we met in places where we ordinarily do not meet them. Apparently, when we attribute knowledge of some kind to some individuals, we can only do so under the assumption that a number of internal conditions in the individual as well as a number of external conditions are such as to make this knowledge available. It is naturally difficult in studies of cognition to ascertain that knowledge attributed to an individual actually is available to the individual. A technique for controlling availability of knowledge in problem solving has been described by the present writer (Saugstad, 1955). The point to be discussed here is the control which the speaker can exert over the knowledge of the listener. When it is borne in mind that knowledge which has once been acquired, and which has been used in a variety of situations, may become unavailable, it is more easily understood that human individuals may have a great use of language as a means of transmitting information in everyday life situations. For example, in a specific situation there may be objects present which an individual has learnt to identify, but which for lack of attention she or he may not be perceiving. By means of language another individual may direct attention to the object. It is, therefore, easy to understand that human individuals living close to nature may benefit greatly from making each other aware of sources of food or of dangers. By means of language human individuals can do that in an efficient manner. Also, due to changes in motivational and emotional states and other conditions affecting alertness, human individuals may not be capable of remembering or recalling objects or events which ordinarily form part of their repertory. By naming the object forgotten, an individual may make it available to another individual. Effects of such naming have been demonstrated in experiments of problem solving. (On this point, see Clark and Clark, ibid). Further, for a variety of reasons human individuals may fail to anticipate or imagine events which may occur in the future and which they ordinarily would be capable of anticipating or imagining. Finally, I shall mention that it may frequently happen that human individuals fail to draw inferences which they have drawn a number of times previously. Apparently, by making reference to events to be anticipated or to inferences which may be drawn, language may be of great help. In the four types of situations I have mentioned, verbal communication may be said to assist human individuals in perceiving the world and in remembering, imagining, and thinking of objects and events previously experienced. Apparently an important—and relatively simple—function of language is that by means of it, it is possible to make knowledge available to other individuals. As the reader will understand, this function is somewhat different from the use we make of language when we inform other individuals about people, landscapes, animals, and plants which they themselves have not experienced or when we teach each other how to perform various tasks or how to organize our knowledge. The use made of language in teaching and instruction is, of course, of the utmost importance, but it must not lead us to overlook that language has vital functions of a simpler, more elementary nature.

The performance of the speaker and the listener

I have now carried through the examination of language and verbal communication to a point where I am ready to account for the performance of the speaker and the listener. According to principles 1, 2, 3, and 4, words may be ascribed a public meaning, a meaning shared by a linguistic community. Now I shall show that by means of the fifth principle it is possible to give an account of how words defined as previously described can function as instruments of communication. In the previous chapters I have argued that the vocabulary is the central part of a language, that the phonological system is primarily a means of creating linguistic signs, and that grammar is a means of making communication more efficient. In the previous chapter I pointed out that the vocabularies of the speakers of a language vary in a quantitative fashion, and that the main problem in accounting for the performance of the speaker and the listener consists in showing that single, isolated linguistic signs may by used for communication. I shall consider first how verbal communication may be carried out by means of isolated linguistic signs. Then in a later section I shall discuss the nature of the sentence.

Because users of language only sometimes—and not oridinarily—communicate by means of isolated words, I shall have to make up some imagined examples. The fact that the examples are imagined does not, of course, make them unrealistic. I shall consider examples which may be illustrative of verbal communication under relatively simple conditions.

I shall begin by assuming that the individuals communicating with each other have a very restricted number of linguistic signs. No assumption is made as to whether the linguistic signs chosen were the signs or type of signs used at the initial stages of the evolution of verbal communication. I shall assume that the individuals have signs for the following four concepts: 'food', 'water', 'danger', and 'child'. I think it is easy to imagine that these signs would be highly useful in a great variety of situations. Suppose for example, that there is a scarcity of food or water and two or more individuals are spread out over a territory in search for these commodities. In this situation it is easy to understand that the use of the first two signs mentioned would be highly useful to the group. It will further be understood that in this type of context it would be relatively clear to a receiver of the sign what information was transmitted by it. The information would be that food was present. In the specific context the information *would not* be that the individual producing it was thinking of the meal she/he had some days ago. Nor would the information be that the individual producing it was thinking of how nice it might be some time in the future to eat or drink. The definite context in which the individuals are situated is of such a nature that it makes possible a specific interpretation by the individuals perceiving the sign. Let us further assume that in this context there were a number of wild and dangerous beasts. When an individual uses the sign for danger the other individuals perceiving the sign would tend to interpret it in the way that some beast was in the neighbourhood. This might be highly important information. Again it will be understood that most likely the individuals perceiving the sign would understand it to refer to a definite type of knowledge, namely that a beast was in the neighbourhood. Let us finally in this or a similar context consider the use that could be made of the sign for 'child'. Suppose a child had been lost. In this type of context the production of the sign would contribute to making the individuals of the group search for the child.

It is thus easy to see that in many instances the use of an isolated sign would be superior to just making some loud noise, say, that of screaming or yelling. The use of the sign would make specific what was to be done or to be expected by the members of the group. *The essential point in the account given above is that in verbal communication the speaker and the listener receive important cues from their reciprocal relationship as well as from the situation, the context, in which they find themselves.* These cues guide speakers when they attempt to transmit information and they guide listeners in their attempt at understanding what definite knowledge the speaker has attempted to impart to them. I shall illustrate the point by another example. Suppose a group of individuals have signs for the concepts 'stone' and 'hammer' and suppose further that an individual tries to crack a nut or a bone without the use of any tool. Located close to the individual is a stone appropriate for being used as a hammer, but this object is either not perceived or the individual does not think of the fact that it can be used as a hammer for cracking the nut or the bone. On noting the activity of this individual another individual may point to the stone and produce a sign for either the concept 'stone' or the concept 'hammer'. In a variety of instances this way of communication, that the stone may be used for hammering, may be entirely adequate. As the readers may verify for themselves, a large number of examples similar to those I have mentioned here might be found in which adequate communication may be achieved by the use of isolated, single signs.

So far I have considered the use of single, isolated signs. Now I shall turn to examples in which the utterance consists of two or more signs produced in succession, but not related to each other by means of grammatical rules. I shall return to the examples where I imagined a group of individuals having signs for 'food', 'water', 'danger', and 'child'. To these four signs I shall add a sign for the fact that some object is distant or that an event takes place at a distance.

Adding the sign 'distant' would tend to make an utterance more precise. For example, in many situations the utterances: "Food, distant" and "Child, distant" may be more precise than the utterances "Food" and "Child". By producing signs in succession it is easy to understand that it would be possible to transmit information of a rather complicated nature in a precise manner. As I see it, there can be no doubt that individuals who were in the possession of a couple of hundred signs would have at their disposal a very effective assembly of instruments for communication even if they were incapable of using the signs according to grammatical rules.

The cues which speakers and listeners derive from their mutual relationship and the situation or the context in which they find themselves, may be more or less useful for the transmittance and the reception of information. However, when account is taken of the fact that verbal communication is a skill which is improved by practice, it is plausible to assume that verbal communication may have a basis in simple types of communications, such as those considered above. I have, to avoid misunderstandings by the examples given above, made no attempt at giving an account of how use of language originated.

The point I am making is that in a large number of instances speakers and listeners are guided by cues which may allow them to communicate efficiently with a restricted vocabulary and without the use of grammatical rules. I am, of course, not saying that the examples given are representative of all instances in which verbal communication is carried out.

In the next section I shall explain why speakers tend to make their utterances in the form of grammatical sentences. While utterances in this form are easier to understand for a listener, I shall hold that words function in principally the same way in sentences as they do in utterances consisting of isolated words. In line with what I have said about the performance of speakers and listeners in this and the preceding sections of the present chapter, I shall describe the performance of speakers in the following way: *Having noted a difference in available knowledge between themselves and another individual (a listener) and wanting to communicate about this difference, they attempt to adjust the knowledge of the other individual to be indentical in some definite respect to their own knowledge by producing a word or a number of words referring to this difference.* The performance of listeners I shall describe thus: *Having noted that the speaker wants to communicate something to them and having perceived the word or the words uttered, they try to relate the meaning of the word(s) to what they believe to represent a difference in available knowledge between themselves and the speaker.*

The sentence is the unit of information

In the preceding sections of the present chapter I have tried to show that in a large variety of situations it is possible to communicate by words which are not related to each other, combined into sentences by means of grammatical rules. I have based my account on the belief that the behaviour of the speaker and listener is guided by extra-linguistic cues which they derive from a consideration of their relationship in the situation in which the utterance is made. If my account is acceptable it probably gives substantial support to the belief that words are instruments for communication. If it can also be shown that it is possible to explain why even if words are the instruments, the sentence can be the unit of speech, I think a substantial argument against the belief has been removed. If this explanation can be made, it seems possible to develop the idea that language is an assembly of instruments into a coherent and fairly consistent theory.

The problem is to explain how words can be the instruments while the sentence is the unit of speech. One might perhaps prefer to say that also the word is a unit of speech. If this way of stating matters is preferred one may formulate the problem as that of accounting for how speech has two different units. To distinguish between the two units I shall prefer to say that the *word is the unit of meaning, while the sentence is the unit of information.*

The issue at stake is whether the sentence should be regarded as forming part of language, or whether it should be regarded as a product of the use of language. I think it is to the credit of Saussure that he was capable of raising this question. As the reader will remember, Saussure seems to have been unwilling to include the sentence in what he termed 'la langue'. He seems to have tended to think that the sentence was a result of 'la parole'. I think Chomsky and his followers missed an essential point when they insisted that language may be defined as a set of sentences. I am not, of course, agreeing with Saussure that language is a system of signs, but I think he was on the right track when he wondered whether the sentence should be excluded from language. Those who insist that sentences are to be included in language regard it as an essential characteristic of language that words are related to each other in grammatical sentences. Those who, like me, will not include sentences, regard it as a characteristic of speech and not of language that speakers tend to form sentences. To argue that sentences do not form part of language one shall have to show that it is possible to explain the tendency in speakers to produce their utterances in the form of sentences as a result of extra-linguistic facts. I shall show that it is highly plausible to believe that speech is guided by cues which make it natural to produce utterances in the form of sentences.

Before I give my explanation of why speakers tend to produce their utterances in the form of sentences, I want to stress that it is possible to speak only of a *tendency* to make utterances in this form. Speakers do frequently produce utterances consisting of single words and frequently they do not complete what appears as the beginning of a sentence. Also, as I mentioned in Chapter 1, there are utterances, such as "Help", "Fire", "Water" which are not easily classified as sentences. Consequently I shall have to formulate the question to be answered in the following way: why do speakers *tend* to produce their utterances in the form of sentences?

By subjecting to an examination what can be meant by saying that an individual has received some information, I think it is possible to understand how an answer to the question can be worked out. At the present state of knowledge about cognitive processes it is not, of course, possible to give a definite answer to this question. I shall give an answer which I think may be regarded as plausible.

Information must, as I have emphasized, represent knowledge which is new to an individual. However, this fact cannot mean that what is regarded as information is not connected with already existing knowledge, old knowledge. This is so, because it does not seem possible to conceive of anything as knowledge unless it is connected with something else. According to this way of looking at matters, transmittance of information to another individual is most appropriately made in the way that reference is made to some knowledge which is new and to some knowledge which is old. Hence, speakers will tend to construct their utterances in such a way that they contain a reference to some knowledge already possessed by the listener and a reference to some knowledge which is new to the listener. Utterances need not always be constructed according to this scheme, because speakers may leave to the listener to understand what is the old knowledge to which the new knowledge is connected. Apparently, it is possible to conceive of the subject of a sentence as the part of the sentence which refers to the old knowledge, and the predicate as the part which refers to the new knowledge or, what may be a preferable way of stating matters, to conceive of that which is talked about as the old knowledge and that which is said about that which is talked about as the new knowledge. If this should be a tenable way of expressing matters, one may say that the main structure of the grammatical sentence corresponds to the way of making utterances which is most appropriate for transmitting information. From this one may infer that speakers will have a tendency to produce utterances in the form of sentences. However, for the reason mentioned there will only be a tendency to produce utterances in the form of sentences and this is in agreement with what is found to be the case.

During the last decades linguists have been increasingly occupied with the problem of accounting for the structure of sentences by taking the point of departure in the assumption that this account can be made in terms of something talked about, and something said about that which is talked about. Charles Hockett (1958) introduced the term 'topic' to refer to that part of a sentence which refers to that which is talked about and the term 'comment' to refer to that part of the sentence which refers to what is said about that which is talked about. The terms are also used in a way, which I think is more adequate, for respectively that which is talked about and that which is said about that which is talked about. Some progress seems to have been made in attempts at accounting for the structure of sentences by means of the terms 'topic' and 'comment' or similar pairs of terms. This is evidence that it is plausible to conceive of the grammatical sentence as a structure which reflects what is the most appropriate way of transmitting information. (A review of work aimed at accounting for the structure of sentences by means of the concepts 'topic' and 'comment' is found in Lyons, 1977.) A discussion of the difficulties involved in stating what are the underlying psychological processes in the construction of sentences according to a scheme involving a topic and a comment, is found in Elisabeth Bates and Brian MacWhinney, 1982.)

Against the position I have taken one may object that even in situations where information might have been given equally well without the use of a grammatical sentence, speakers of a language tend to prefer this form of utterance. Why should they prefer this form if the basis for using sentences is found in the requirements for communication? It is easy to find situations in which requirements for communication would not need a grammatical sentence. For example, one may imagine a situation in which a person informs another by means of an utterance in the form of the grammatical sentence, "The man runs". Why, one may ask, do English speakers express themselves in this way and not, for example, by uttering, "Man run"? I think this objection may be met by reference to the fact that most likely communication will tend to be most efficient when information is given in a standard form and the sentence is a form which is highly appropriate. Hence, even if requirements to communication do not in all situations need utterances in the form of grammatical sentences, the sentence as a better way of transmitting information than other ways, will be preferred. Also, it is of course advantageous to speakers that they can make most of their utterances in a standard form because this may make their work easier. Apparently, the fact that in a majority of instances speakers of a language tend to produce utterances in the form of sentences, cannot be taken as an argument that sentences belong to language and not merely to speech.

As units of information in verbal communication, sentences must be defined with reference to three different types of knowledge: 1. knowledge about the meanings of the particular linguistic signs making up the sentence, 2. knowledge of requirements to transmittance of information, and 3. knowledge about the rules for making grammatical sentences in the language of the speaker. As the reader will understand, at the present state of knowledge it is not possible to define in a precise and general manner the term 'sentence'.

In connection with the problem of defining a sentence it must be stressed that from the fact that sentences cannot be defined in terms only of semantic considerations it does not follow that it is possible to define them with regard *only* to the grammatical rules of the language of the speaker. In his *Syntactic Structures* Chomsky (1957, pp. 15—17) seems to have made this inference. He rightly pointed out that there are no semantic reasons why certain types of utterances are regarded as grammatical while other types of utterances are not. However, from this fact he jumped to the conclusion that semantic considerations are of no relevance in attempts at characterizing grammatical sentences. 'Grammar', he declared, is autonomous and independent of meaning. Of course, grammar is *not* independent of meaning. When Chomsky started out parsing sentences he began by dividing them into 'noun phrases' and 'verb phrases'. One may wonder how it is possible to decide what is meant by a 'noun phrase' and a 'verb phrase' unless notions of meaning are invoked. Apparently, Chomsky failed to give his idea of grammar a basis in empirical facts, that is in reality.

Related to the question of whether sentences should be regarded as belonging to language is the question whether sentences have meaning. I have argued that utterances in the form of sentences are means of transmitting information. The information they transmit is dependent upon not only the linguistic signs making up the utterance, but also upon the relationship between the speaker and the listener. As communicatory acts the information they transmit will, therefore, depend upon the particular individuals who are participating in the act. Also, because the information transmitted depends on the specific situation in which the speaker and listener find themselves when the utterance is made, the information transmitted may vary when the situation changes, even if the speaker and the listener are the same. According to this way of looking at matters, it seems difficult to conceive of a standard set of speakers and listeners, and a standard situation in which an utterance in the form of a sentence might obtain a specific, a definite meaning. In everyday speech one sometimes distinguishes between the literal meaning and the actual meaning of an utterance. For example, one may distinguish between a literal and an actual meaning when someone utters the sentence, "The door is open", with the intention to make somebody shut the door. From the fact that it sometimes is possible to distinguish between what might be an unusual and a more literal meaning of an utterance, it does not, of course, follow that utterances in the form of sentences have meaning. As I have argued, this belief is highly dubious.

John Austin (1961) argued emphatically that sentences, but not words, have meaning. His belief that sentences have meaning seems to underlie his famous attempts at drawing a distinction between utterances referred to respectively as 'locutionary' and 'illocutionary acts' (Austin, 1962). By the former type of acts he had in mind utterances which had a more or less definite sense, as, for example, the sentence, "The door is open" used to refer to a particular door, and by the latter type the act one may perform when one performs the locutionary act. If one asks under what circumstances an individual would utter a sentence such as the one mentioned, it seems to me that it would always be done to perform in some way by performing it. One might, for example, utter it in reply to a question, to express surprise or alarm. I have difficulties in seeing that these ways of using the sentence differ principally from the use aimed at making someone shut the door. I think Austin one-sidedly examined linguistic problems from the view of the speaker, leaving out of consideration the listener. I shall hold that in order to understand what act is performed one must examine the relationship between the speaker and the listener in the particular situation in which utterances are made.

On the nature of grammar

Sentences, I have argued, are the products of the use made of language and should not be regarded as forming part of language. However, even if sentences were not included in language, the rules for forming grammatical sentences might be included. When words are regarded as instruments I think it is natural to *consider grammatical rules as rules for the use of the instruments*. I shall show that this view of language is in agreement with what is known about the speech of the peoples of the world.

It is known that speakers of all languages use grammatical rules. In the previous section I argued that the sentence must be regarded as the preferred way of transmitting verbal information. To make transmittance of information more efficient, rules for the formation of sentences are useful. However, because there can be no way of forming a sentence which guarantees that information is transmitted, no rule can be regarded as absolutely necessary for verbal communication. Therefore, it is not to be expected that speakers of all languages should use the same rules. This view is in accordance with the fact that none of the rules found in the diverse languages are used by speakers of all languages, in other words no rule for the formation of sentences is universal.

I shall show that it is possible to argue convincingly for the belief that grammatical rules are the rules for the use of the instruments, i.e. for the use of words. Traditionally philologists and linguists have distinguished between morphology and syntax. 'Morphology' is that part of the study of grammar which concerns patterns of word formation and 'syntax', the part which concerns relationships between words in sentences. According to this way of dividing grammar a distinction must be drawn between morphological and syntactical rules. I shall consider both types of grammatical rules. Because I have already dealt with problems of sentence formation I shall begin by discussing syntactical rules.

The use of syntactical rules may be illustrated by the rule of congruence followed by speakers of English that verbs in the present tense must conform to the subject. When the subject is in the third person this must be marked by the ending *s* in the verb. This rule may be regarded as an instruction to the listener to regard the verb as being related to the word or the phrase denoting the subject of the sentence. Another illustration of the use of syntactical rules is the word order to be followed in declarative sentences of the English language. In this type of sentences the verb is to follow the word or the phrase denoting the subject of the sentence. This may be taken as an instruction to the listener to regard a particular word or a particular phrase as referring to the subject of the sentence. I think the point I have illustrated by the two syntactical rules discussed here holds true for all other types of syntactical rules, and I shall turn to the morphological rules.

The first question I shall deal with is why there should be morphological rules. In Chapter 6 I argued that words which are common names are defined with a reference to concepts. The concept is the characteristic which defines membership in a certain category. In line with this reasoning a name denotes only a particular characteristic of the objects communicated about. For example, the name 'tree' denotes only the concept 'tree', i.e. the characteristic which determines membership in the category 'tree'. It does not denote whether one or more members of the category is meant. The listener may infer this from the context. However, it may be convenient to make clear what is meant by the use of a specific sign and speakers of a number of languages do that. For example, speakers of the English language denote that a plurality is meant by adding the inflectional ending *s* to most nouns. The adding of this ending may be taken as an instruction to the listener that the noun is to be understood as referring to a plurality of instances, to more than one member of a category. To give another example, the use of the ending *ed* to mark the past tense of English regular verbs may be taken as an instruction to the listener to conceive of the action as taking place in the past. To give a third example, which, even if it may not strictly be considered a morphological rule of the *English* language, illustrates the point I am making: the use of the definite article *the* may be regarded as an instruction to the listener to consider a noun or a composite phrase to refer to a definite instance or to definite instances of some kind. It is easy to see that such rules for the use of words of the type 'common names' can be useful. However, because these rules are not necessary for the understanding of verbal utterances it is not to be expected that they should be universal, i.e. used by speakers of all languages. As a matter of fact they are not. Speakers of some languages may, for example, not denote the plural and speakers of some other languages not the definite instance. From what I have said, I think it can be understood that also morphological rules can be regarded as rules for the use of instruments.

Languages have a variety of rules for denoting grammatical relationships and a variety of signs for denoting such rules. The distinction between these signs and words is not always clear-cut, but it is ordinarily not difficult to draw the distinction between the two types of signs. It will be noted that a definition of signs used to denote grammatical rules cannot be made with a reference only to extra-linguistic facts, but must also include a reference to words.

Before I leave the discussion of morphology I want to add a remark on the fact mentioned in Chapter 1, that words may have different forms. When it is assumed—as I have done—that words are defined with a reference to definite extra-linguistic entities, it is not so difficult to understand that they are identifiable even if their form has been changed by adding to them various types of prefixes, suffixes, and infixes. Adding to a word a sign which denotes some rule for the use of the word is evidently an efficient way of marking that in the use of the word a specific rule is to be followed. Hence, according to this way of looking at matters, it is not so difficult to understand that words may have a variety of forms and sometimes a complicated structure.

If it is correct that grammatical rules are most adequately conceived of as rules for effective communication, it seems to follow that in order to clarify their nature one cannot concentrate only on the structure of language, but must consider also the use made of it. As I argued in Chapter 1, in a productive study of language, structure must be related to function and function to structure. To study the function of grammatical rules one must study how information is transmitted by means of language. Until more is understood of this transmittance it is difficult to understand more precisely what can be meant by an adequate description of the grammar of a particular language.

Use of language is a skill

An individual using an instrument can only do so when she or he is in the possession of a skill. By emphasizing that language is an instrument I also emphasize that the use of it is a skill, and a very complicated skill. In order to master it an individual must be capable of understanding the meaning of the signs used in the utterances and of producing the signs. Moreover, as I have emphasized in the present chapter, in order to communicate effectively by means of language, an individual must have an extensive knowledge of the thinking and behaviour of other individuals. Because this thinking and behaviour reflect the culture of the speech community, as emphasized by Hymes (ibid) and Gumperz (ibid), communicative competence cannot be achieved unless the individual has acquired knowledge of the culture of the speech community.

As might be expected, children learn to master the skill of using language by a long and laborious process. When at the age of five to six years they have acquired a substantial vocabulary and have learnt the grammatical rules of their language, they still have to learn a number of new words and new ways of expressing their own knowledge as well as of adjusting the knowledge of other individuals. The skill of using language is improved throughout a large part of the life of human individuals, and some individuals may improve their skill throughout all of their lives.

As might be expected, one finds considerable individual variations in the individuals' skill in using language, and, as Hymes (ibid) has pointed out, different cultures may attach different importance to the skill of using language. Thus there may be differences in the skill of using language between peoples of different cultures.

When it is taken into consideration that verbal communication is learnt through a long and laborious process, it will be understood that by a study of the use of language in adult individuals one can obtain only a highly restricted understanding of linguistic performance. As argued by Vygotsky (ibid), to make this study a productive one scientists must study how the skill develops in the individual. This study must, as insisted by Jerome Bruner (1983, p. 103), take its point of departure in the fact that "children learn to use a language initially (or its prelinguistic precursors) to get what they want, to play games, to stay connected with those on whom they are dependent". In other words, a study of the skill of using language must begin by studying how children establish social relationships to other individuals and how they acquire the culture of their speech community.

Chapter 8

The model and linguistic reality

Mögen andere kommen die es besser machen.

Ludwig Wittgenstein, *Tractatus Logico-Philosophicus*, Vorwort des Verfassers, 1921.

In Chapter 4 I discussed procedures for constructing scientific theories. I concluded that in fields not yet structured by theory the procedure to be followed must consist in: 1. a delimitation of the field of research and 2. an ordering of the items (the facts and putative facts) assumed to be contained in the field. In line with this conclusion in Chapters 5–7 I have delimited a field of linguistic research and have suggested a way of ordering the field. The delimitation and the ordering of the field represents a theoretical model which gives a picture of knowledge about language, a picture of what I shall refer to as 'linguistic reality'. If the model is accepted as a plausible way of depicting linguistic reality, it will represent a means of determining what is to be regarded as important problems in the study of language.

In Chapter 4 I argued that there is no simple way in which the adequacy of a scientific theory can be evaluated. Theoretical models are ways of ordering certain items and there can be no rule which tells how precise the concepts used for this ordering ought to be, or how rigorously relationships ought to be stated. Precision and rigour must be as high as circumstances allow. Because the freedom of the theorists is constrained by the items contained in the field, it is hardly possible to decide how much freedom they have to make their models suggestive for research. This means that it is hardly possible to evaluate the usefulness of a model in terms of its suggestiveness for research. Ideally a theory ought to explain all known facts, but it may take a long time before this ideal is approximated. Also, it may frequently be difficult to understand why a theory does not explain a certain fact. Hence, theories cannot simply be discarded because they do not explain all facts.

However, even if there are no simple rules according to which scientific theories can be evaluated, there are procedures which are useful in attempts at producing knowledge which may lead to improvements of a theory or to the construction of alternative theories. By subjecting to a careful examination facts which it seems plausible to believe a given theory should explain, one may improve the theory or find ways of constructing a better one. Moreover, scientists may try to consider implications of the theory for research in new areas. Such research may produce knowledge which helps to give the theory a broader basis, or which makes clear that the theory is lacking in coherence or consistency. In the present chapter I shall repeat what I regard as the main points of the theory. Then I shall consider certain facts which I think it ought to explain and then finally I shall indicate how the theory can be made relevant to two important areas of linguistic research: the study of the phylo- and ontogenetic development.

Summary and evaluation of the model

In Chapters 1 and 2 I adduced evidence for the beliefs that thinking has evolved and takes place independently of language and that language has a basis in perception and thinking. In line with these beliefs I argued in Chapters 5 and 6 that it is highly plausible that the basis for word-meaning can be found in the structure of perception and thinking. In Chapter 7 I showed that words defined by reference to the structure of perception and thinking can be used for communication. In Chapter 3 I argued that use of language must be regarded as a form of behaviour, and in Chapter 7 I described the behaviour involved in verbal communication.

I have insisted that in order to understand the nature of language it is essential to make clear what is its basis in perception and thinking. It should be noted that the taking of this position does not preclude the possibility that once acquired language may affect man's thinking. In Chapter 2 I mentioned that Vygotsky may have suggested a plausible explanation of how language may contribute to the development of the capacity for thinking.

The scientific study of language will not be placed on a firm footing until scientists have produced an acceptable theory of cognition. To avoid unnecessary misunderstandings I want the reader to note that I have merely expressed certain views concerning the structure of cognition and the relationships between, on the one hand, perception and thinking and, on the other, language. At best these views represent certain beliefs which may form part of a theory of cognition. Hence, the construction of the model is no attempt at giving a coherent and consistent account of the relationship between the use of language and other cognitive activities.

In this book I have argued that it is not possible to describe the structure of language adequately without also describing its use. Hence, I reject the belief of Saussure that it is possible to have a science of language which is limited to 'la langue' as well as the belief of Chomsky that a productive study of language can be made by concentrating on what he referred to as 'competence'. A productive study of language must include at one time 'la langue' and 'la parole' , or 'competence' and 'performance'. The inclusion of respectively 'la parole' and the 'performance' in the study of language raises the problem of specifying what are the essential functions of language. As I have shown, this problem must be viewed in the perspective of the phylo- and ontogenetic development. I have tried to adduce evidence for the belief that the primary function of language is communication. Even if this belief is widely accepted it is essential to find support for it and to specify it in a more precise manner. As I have pointed, out, scientists believing that language has evolved as a means of thinking must take the burden of showing how language has acquired this function. Also, because it is a fact that language serves as a means of communication, they must explain how language having evolved as a means of thinking has come to serve as a means of communication.

The central idea of the present approach is that language is an assembly of words which serve as instruments for communication. The words obtain their meaning from reference to the categories making up man's knowledge. Words are divided into common and proper names. 'Common names' are defined by reference to the characteristics which determine memberships in the categories and 'proper names' are defined by reference to specific members of definite categories. It is assumed that words derive their meaning from a reference to facts of an extra-linguistic nature and not through their use in verbal communication.

In the present approach the vocabulary is regarded as the central part of language. Phonology is a means of producing the items of the vocabulary and grammar is conceived of as rules making communication by means of words more efficient. Hence, to understand the nature of language one must begin by studying the role played by the words.

To develop the central idea into a model which in a coherent and consistent manner can account for language and its use, it has been necessary to show that words can be defined with reference to an extra-linguistic cognitive basis. Moreover, it has been necessary to explain how words so defined can be used for communication. The explanation I have worked out for the transmittance of information is based upon the idea that the relationship the speaker and the listener have to each other provides them with essential cues for respectively transmitting and receiving information. These cues derive from the fact that transmittance of information presupposes that there is a difference in available knowledge between the speaker and the listener. Accordingly, the goal of the speaker is to adjust the knowledge of the listener to be identical in some definite respect to her/his own knowledge and the goal of the listener is to have her/his knowledge adjusted to be identical in some definite respect to that of the speaker's. A consideration of their reciprocal relationship will in a variety of situations provide the speaker and the listener with essential cues for respectively transmitting and receiving information.

According to this way of looking at matters 'information' as transmitted in verbal communication must be defined with reference to the relationship between the speaker and the listener. From this it follows that the informational value of a verbal utterance cannot be determined by an examination or analysis only of the meaning of the linguistic signs making up the utterance. In line with this conclusion I have drawn a distinction between a unit of meaning and a unit of information. I have suggested that the word (the name) represents the unit of meaning and the sentence the unit of information. Grammar, I have suggested, are rules for making communication with words more efficient. Hence, to understand the nature of grammar one must understand how communication is carried out with words. Grammarians have studied grammar for hundreds of years, but seem to have devoted little attention to this problem. As a result, the study of grammar has remained a formal study empty of content.

Grammatical rules are of a variety of types and a number of different types of morphemes are used to designate these rules. Traditionally the rules have been divided into syntactical and morphological rules. The distinction is important and in the previous chapter I accounted for the difference between the two sets of rules.

In Chapter 6 I mentioned that the fact that words may be used metaphorically does not contradict the belief that words are defined with reference to definite extra-linguistic entities. When it is observed that a distinction can be drawn between the way a word is defined and the way it is used in communication, it is understood that words can be used in a metaphorical manner. Also it will be understood that the belief that words are defined by reference to specific entities is not contradicted by the fact of polysemy. To reconcile the fact of polysemy with the belief that words are defined by reference to specific entities, one need only assume that speakers can keep in mind a definition originally given of a word while they associate the word with different entities. That they can do this is not difficult to understand when account is taken of the fact that most likely new meanings arise in a word when the word has been used for some time and that in learning a word an individual may learn one meaning at a time.

Later in this chapter I shall show that the model can give a plausible account of the phylogenetic development of language and that it seems to be in close agreement with facts concerning the ontogenetic development of language. Here I shall mention that what is known about similarities and differences found between languages seems to be in line with what can be expected from the model. When it is assumed that thinking and use of language are different things and that language is an expression of thoughts, it is easy to understand that speakers have considerable freedom in constructing verbal utterances, and groups of individuals living apart may express themselves in different ways. Because languages change over time, after a lengthy period of time differences between them may become considerable. It will be noted that while it is easy to reconcile the model with the fact that languages undergo changes with the passing of time, the model cannot explain how these changes take place. To give a coherent and consistent account of how and why languages differ from each other it would have to be combined with a theory of how language changes over periods of time. In Chapter 1 I mentioned that at the beginning of the 20th century outstanding scholars argued that a scientific study of language had to be carried out along historical lines. Apparently this view is too extreme, but it must still be regarded as highly plausible that various differences between languages must be explained by reference to their history.

In the model the phonological system is assumed primarily to be a means of producing discrete linguistic signs. While this view is consistent with the basic assumptions of the model, it must be noted that the model *cannot* explain why all languages have a basis in a phonological system. To obtain a deeper understanding of the role played by the phonological system, one shall probably have to explain why all languages have this basis. As Gordon Hewes (1976) has argued, it is plausible to believe that language has originated in manual gestures. If this view should be correct, it may possibly not be a central fact about language that it has a phonological basis. That it is not, is also suggested by the fact that individuals born deaf may learn to communicate extremely effectively by manual signs. On the other hand, the fact that all known languages have a phonological basis suggests that it is an essential feature of language.

By assuming that thinking and language are different activities one can also understand that speakers may exhibit individual differences in their choice of words and in their preference for the use of specific grammatical rules. Because human individuals have different interests, motivations, and also different opportunities for practising verbal communication, one may expect considerable individual differences in speech.

Phylogenetic development of language

Even if we do not know how language evolved in man's phylogenesis, it must be regarded as a fact that it has evolved and a model of language must explain how this evolution has taken place. The model presented attempts an explanation of this fact which may be useful for research.

The model is based on the belief that the main difference between language and the forms of communication found in the non-human primate species is that language presupposes a capacity for understanding that concepts can be named and that names can be used for communication. As I have made clear, even a very restricted number of names might be of great usefulness to a group of individuals. Hence, if individuals of a group were able to acquire the use of a few names, they might have made the first decisive step towards verbal communication. From what we know about the capacity chimpanzees have for learning to use linguistic signs, it is highly plausible to believe that the capacity for using names may not be far beyond their capacity. Hence, it may not be so difficult to understand that our ancestors could acquire the capacity for using symbols for communication.

In connection with the point made above a suggestion by Geschwind (1969) may be of interest. Geschwind speculated that the angular gyrus region in man played a central role in naming. This region might make associations between visual and tactile sensory impressions and symbolic auditory presentation more easy. Hence, the evolution of this part of the cortex might explain that our ancestors could acquire a capacity for naming which made their communication different from that of other primate species. In making his suggestion Geschwind also made clear that activity in the angular gyrus seems to be relatively independent of the activity of the limbic system which seems to be closely related to the expression of affects. The role played by the angular gyrus may thus help to explain how verbal communication may have become more independent of the expression of emotions. (For a discussion of Geschwind's hypothesis, see John Limber, 1980.) If Geschwind's speculations should have a factual basis, it is possible to explain the acquisition of the use of symbols for communication in terms of a *relatively* small increase in cortical tissue.

In the previous chapter I emphasized that the increase in vocabulary may have taken place more or less gradually. At present we have fairly good evidence that in the adult individual Wernicke's area plays a role in associating meaning to the auditory representation of linguistic signs. Hence, it is possible that this area allowed our ancestors to increase their vocabulary.

In the model, grammar is conceived of as representing merely a supplement to the vocabulary. Still, the capacity for using grammatical rules may be regarded as an important step in the evolution of language. Hence, it is not implausible to believe that a specific area evolved, which helped to express relationships in a more efficient manner. In Chapter 1 I mentioned that some neurophysiologists believed that Broca's area played a role in the expression of syntactic relationships. This belief is plausible and, if it could be shown to be true, it might explain how the capacity for grammar had been made possible by the addition of new cortical tissue. If Broca's area really is responsible for the capacity for expressing grammatical relationships, one might derive from the model the prediction that *Broca's area has evolved later than Wernicke's area.* In considering this possibility it must be noted that there can be no clear-cut line of division between semantics and grammar.

A central point in the model presented is that verbal communication proceeds in the way in which the speaker adjusts the knowledge available to the listener. As I have emphasized, in order to be capable of adjusting the knowledge of another individual, speakers must be capable of registering differences in knowledge between themselves and other individuals.

Evidently, a capacity for registering such differences is dependent upon highly developed intellectual capacities. However, it is also reasonable to believe that this capacity is dependent upon extensive interaction with other individuals and hence that it reflects a particularly tight social organization. If this line of reasoning is sound we should expect that the capacity for language in addition to intellectual capacities involves a specific social relationship between the individuals which make up the speech community. According to this way of looking at matters one reason why the great apes have not developed more advanced means of communication, is, as I pointed out elsewhere (Saugstad, 1980), that their social structure is not tight enough to develop a capacity for the use of language. Since I made my point Savage-Rumbaugh and her collaborators have discovered that the pygmy chimpanzee (*Pan paniscus*) seems to have a greater capacity for communication by means of symbols than the species *Pan troglodytes.* (This finding I discussed in Chapter 1.) The *Pan paniscus* seems also to be a more social animal than the other species of chimpanzee (Alison Badrian and Noel Badrian, 1984). Savage-Rumbaugh et al. (1985, b) report that the *Pan paniscus* is an exceedingly gregarious animal, further that it possesses a larger and more flexible gestural and vocal repertoire than the common chimpanzee and that it engages in patterns of eye contact that are more human in form, and still further that the female copulates throughout the cycle. Mention may also be made of the fact that ventro-ventral copulation is common. If the *Pan paniscus* is a more social animal, this may help to explain why it has a greater capacity for communication. If this should turn out to be correct it may come close to a prediction from my theoretical position which was presented prior to the study of communication in the pygmy chimpanzee.

In Chapter 1 I mentioned the view advanced by Hymes that the study of language must take its point of departure in the study of a speech community. The point I have made concerning the capacity for registering differences in knowledge may be regarded as complementary to his conceptions of the social nature of language.

Ontogenetic development of language

To avoid unnecessary misunderstandings I shall emphasize that I shall make no attempt to give a coherent account of how children acquire use of language. I shall show that the model can account for what appears to be some of the main facts of language development in children. Also, I shall indicate what seem to be certain interesting implications of the model.

It is a widely accepted view that the first utterances of children are in the form of single, isolated signs. These signs seem more or less to correspond to the words contained in the language of the speech community to which the child belongs. As I have emphasized, verbal communication can take place by means of single, isolated signs. It is natural to believe that this is the simplest form of verbal communication and consequently that the child's first utterances contain only single, isolated signs. If this view is correct, it is important to stress that the first utterances should not be regarded as abbreviated sentences or holophrases. It seems most appropriate to term them 'one-word utterances'.

After having passed through a stage where children produce one-word utterances they seem to arrive at a stage in which they use two words together. In the previous chapter I argued that as a result of the fact that man's knowledge is structured in a certain manner, transmittance of information will tend to take place in the way that utterances will be of a form in which two words are related to each other. Hence, according to the theory presented it is to be expected that the second stage in language development in children will be one in which they tend to use two words in juxtaposition.

Grammar, I have argued, is a supplement to the vocabulary. Grammatical rules can be formed only after an individual has begun to use a number of words. Hence, it is to be expected that the child begins to follow grammatical rules when for some time it has used two words in juxtaposition. I have also argued that no grammatical rule is necessary for verbal communication, and that the removal or addition of a rule does not necessarily affect the other grammatical rules of the language. Therefore, it is to be expected that the child tends to learn one rule at a time, and this seems to be in agreement with the facts.

In the remaining part of the chapter I shall show how the model may further help improve present understanding of language acquisition in the child.

The activity involved in the use of language has two apparent characteristics. 1. It requires highly developed intellective capacities and 2. is rooted in man's social life. Scientists and philosophers have elaborated on these two characteristics in a number of ways. However, few seem to have realized that what is distinctive about use of language is that the two characteristics interact so closely that they may be said to fuse. As

I argued in the previous chapter, the goal of the speaker is to adjust a difference in knowledge between herself/himself and a listener, and the goal of the listener is to have this difference adjusted. Evidently highly intellective capacities are required in order that an individual shall be able to note differences in knowledge between herself/himself and fellow individuals. Also, it seems equally evident that in order to note such differences an individual must have extensive experience with the reactions of fellow individuals, and this experience must be the result of a close social relationship to other individuals. When language is looked upon in this manner it becomes apparent that in order to understand how it is acquired in ontogenesis, it is necessary to study the development of the intellective capacities of the child as well as the way in which the child acquires its social relationships.

While for close to one hundred years psychologists have made extensive studies of the intellective development of the child, they seem to have devoted little attention to the problem of how children learn to note differences in knowledge between themselves and other individuals. It is natural to believe that an important foundation for the capacity for noting differences in knowledge is laid in the period in which the child is closely dependent upon its caretakers. In this period the child is dependent upon the reactions of other individuals and interacts extensively with them. Piaget (1926) held that up to the age of 6—7 children had difficulties in taking the perspective of other individuals. In Piaget's terms the child is 'egocentric'. Piaget's concept 'egocentric' is unclear and he seems to have exaggerated the inability of the young child to take the perspective of other individuals. When account is taken of the fact that early in their development children do probably experience conflicts between their needs and the reactions in the caretakers, and that at an early age they learn to express their needs and to cooperate with other individuals, it is natural to believe that the capacity for noting differences in knowledge between themselves and other individuals develops at a much earlier stage than apparently assumed by Piaget. Actually, by studying how children learn to use the definite and the indefinite articles, child psychologists have been able to accumulate information which helps them to trace this development. The point of departure is taken from the fact that the indefinite article tends to be used when reference is made to something not known to the listener, and the definite article, when something is known to the listener or has been referred to previously. So, in order to master the use of the definite and the indefinite article, the child must understand what is known to other individuals. Hence, this mastery reflects children's capacity for noting differences between themselves and other individuals. (For an interesting review of the study of children's use of the indefinite and the definite articles, see Clark and Clark, ibid.) More recently Macnamara (1982) has argued rather convincingly that at the age of three children seem to have a good mastery of the use of definite and indefinite articles. This suggests that at this age children must have a highly developed capacity for registering differences in knowledge between themselves and other individuals.

Below I shall suggest a procedure which may produce an answer to the question I have raised concerning the role played in language acquisition by the capacity for noting the type of differences discussed. Here I want to draw attention to the fact that there is some evidence which indicates that use of language is closely dependent upon the capacity for establishing social relationships. Children exhibiting what is known as Kanner's autism may have well-developed intellective capacities, but may not form normal social relationships. They are frequently poor speakers. More recently Macnamara (ibid) has found evidence which indicates that children suffering from this type of autism may have particular difficulties in learning the use of personal pronouns. As he pointed out, in order to understand the reference of personal pronouns an individual must have analyzed the relationship between speakers and listeners. Earlier in the present chapter I mentioned that *Pan paniscus* seems to have a tighter social organization and a greater capacity for communication by means of symbols. This may be taken as an indication that the capacity for use of language is closely dependent upon the development of social relationships.

According to the model presented verbal communication depends upon a capacity for adjusting differences in knowledge between oneself and other individuals and upon a capacity for having one's knowledge adjusted by other individuals. Hence, in addition to having a capacity for noting differences in knowledge of the type discussed, speakers and listeners must have a capacity for adjusting the knowledge of other individuals and for having their own knowledge adjusted by means of linguistic signs. As I stressed in Chapters 3 and 7, little is known about the way speakers and listeners perform in verbal communication. However, I think it is natural to believe that communication in which the knowledge of an individual is adjusted by means of linguistic signs represents a continuation of forms of communication acquired earlier by the child. As we all know, prior to the onset of speech children communicate by crying, smiling, moving towards objects, by gestures, eye-movements, movements of arms, and by pointing. Following these more primitive forms of communication there may be a period in which children use signs which substitute the primitive forms, but which do not obtain their meaning from a reference to concepts. Signs of this type are: *Hi*, *Bye-bye*, *There*, *Here*, *See*. These utterances are usually accompanied by movements. They may be acquired by associative learning, and because they are not defined by reference to categories in the way described in Chapter 6 I shall not regard them as names, that is words.

I have emphasized that when the child begins to communicate by means of names, it has taken the most important step in language acquistion. However, it must be noted that communication by means of names—even if they are not related to each other by grammatical rules—is a most complicated process. In Chapter 1, in discussing biology and language, I mentioned that Lenneberg had argued that names are not acquired by simple associative learning. In that section I also reported the results of attempts at teaching chimpanzees communication by means of symbols which showed that the use of names could hardly be acquired by associative learning. A particularly convincing argument against the belief that children learn words in this way has been made by Macnamara (ibid). As he made clear, personal pronouns, such as *I* and *You* are acquired *early* in the child's acquisition of language. Personal pronouns are used for different individuals and, therefore, cannot be learnt by associating specific signs to specific individuals. Apparently, if the capacity for using names is regarded as a requirement to speech, speaking demands highly developed cognitive capacities. In this connection it should be mentioned that Piaget may have made an important point concerning language acquisition when he observed that speech appeared at a time at which the child's capacity for forming representations seemed to increase rapidly, i.e. at a time at which the child's capacity for remembering and drawing increased and at which the child engaged in symbolic play. (On this point, see Piaget and Barbara Inhelder, 1969.)

In an attempt at accounting for the learning of names by children, it seems essential to answer the following question: Is it conceivable that children will learn a number of names without having some understanding that names can be used for communication? Granting that there is a connection between the learning of names and the understanding that names are used for communication, one may further ask if there is a connection between the understanding that verbal communication aims at adjusting differences in knowledge and the learning of names. If there is such a connection one should expect that at the time children understand that names can be used for communication, i.e. for adjusting the knowledge of other individuals, their learning of names will increase rapidly. In other words, at the time at which children begin using signs as names and not merely as substitutes for signals used in more primitive forms of communication, their vocabulary should extend quickly. This hypothesis can be investigated empirically. If it should turn out to be tenable, it would help to tie together the perceptual-cognitive and the social aspects involved in language acquistion; this would provide a broader basis for the model I have presented.

Actually, there may be some evidence in support of the hypothesis discussed above. In the study of his son's language acquisition, Halliday (1975) noted that at a certain period of time the child would produce names without any apparent attempt at transmitting information. Following this period there was a rapid increase in the use of names for communication. Children seem to pass through a period in which they produce words without an apparent intent to communicate anything. If this period is followed by a rapid increase in the vocabulary it may be taken as evidence that in this period they begin to understand that names have a use.

The study of the growth in communicative competence in the child is complicated by the fact that long before children are capable of being able to articulate words and use them for communication they seem to be capable of understanding a variety of verbal utterances. Obviously in some way their capacity for transmitting information must depend on their capacity for understanding speech. However, this fact should not blind us to the possibility that speaking and listening may be somewhat different capacities which may develop relatively independently of each other. In the fifth principle I stated that the goal of the speakers is to adjust the knowledge of the listener while the goal of the listener is to have her/his knowledge adjusted. So, clearly, their goals are different. Elsewhere (Saugstad, 1980) I have likened the difference between speaking and listening to that of throwing and catching a ball. Just as an individual may be relatively better or poorer to throw than to catch a ball, an individual may be relatively better to speak than to listen and vice versa. There is some evidence that the capacities for speaking and listening develop relatively independently of each other. Premack (1986) has adduced some evidence for this view and has suggested that in an early phase comprehension and production of speech are separated. Actually, the difference between the activities of speaking and listening may manifest itself in the way children tend to imitate utterances when asked to do this. As noted by Susan Ervin-Tripp (1964), at the two-word stage children will never imitate new constructions. They will give an utterance back in the form they use in their own utterances. This is explainable by assuming that speaking and listening are different kinds of activities. In connection with the finding of Ervin-Tripp, which has been corroborated by other psychologists, it is interesting to note that children imitate words, but not grammatical constructions they do not themselves use. (For a review of these findings, see Clark and Clark, ibid). This is what may be expected from my model. Use of words is an activity which can be distinguished from the activity of constructing grammatical sentences. According to my position grammar is a supplement to the use of words and must be acquired in practicing the skill of using words. This may explain why children imitate words, but not grammatical constructions when they are asked to repeat utterances of adult speakers.

The present model is based upon knowledge about perception and thinking. As a result of the fact that at present our knowledge of cognition is highly incoherent, it is difficult to state the five principles making up the core of the model in a more precise and rigorous manner. Still, I think the model may prove useful. The linguistic phenomena presenting themselves for empirical research are so closely related to each other that it is difficult to evaluate the plausibility of claims to knowledge unless the relationship between the diverse types of knowledge is specified in a theoretical model. As I hope to have shown in the previous chapters, light can be shed on a number of claims to knowledge by viewing them in the perspective given by the model. Also, I think the model may help to clarify what are the most essential problems for present linguistic research. Finally, as I hope to have shown in the present chapter, the model may present suggestions for the formulation of new research problems which may give some promise of providing useful new knowledge about language.

To make it possible for other scientists to improve the model, I have tried to state as explicitly as possible my position to a number of problems. The model can be improved by a systematic discussion of what facts are to be included and which are to be excluded from the field of linguistic research. Also, it can be improved by stating in a more coherent and consistent manner than I have been able to do the relationship between what are regarded as facts and putative facts. The model may be further improved by approaching the study of language with more productive ideas of scientific procedures than are currently available.

List of References

Alston, W. P. Meaning. In P. Edwards (ed.), *The Encyclopedia of Philosophy*, **5**. New York: Macmillan, 1967, pp. 233–241.

Arbib, M. A. and Caplan, D. Neurolinguistics must be computational. *The Behavioral and Brain Sciences*, **2**, 1979, 449–483.

Austin, J. L. *Philosophical Papers*. Oxford: Oxford University Press, 1961.

Austin, J. L. *How to do Things with Words*. Oxford: Oxford University Press, 1962.

Badrian, A. and Badrian, N. Social organization of *Pan paniscus* in the Lomako Forest, Zaire. In R. L. Susman (ed.), *The Pygmy Chimpanzee*. New York: Plenum Press, 1984, pp. 325–346.

Barwise, J. and Perry, J. *Situations and Attitudes*. Cambridge, Mass.: M.I.T. Press, 1983.

Bates, E. and MacWinney, B. Functionalist approaches to grammar. In E. Wanner and L. Gleitman (eds.), *Language Acquisition: The State of the Art*. Cambridge: Cambridge University Press, 1982, pp. 173–218.

Bateson, G. *Mind and Nature*. New York: Dutton, 1979.

Berlin, B. and Kay, P. *Basic Colour Terms: Their Universality and Evolution*. Berkeley and Los Angeles: University of California Press, 1969.

Bickerton, D. *Roots of Language*. Ann Arbor: Karoma, 1981.

Bloom, L. *One Word at a Time: The Use of Single Word Utterances before Syntax*. The Hague: Mouton, 1973.

Bloomfield, L. *Language*. London: Allen & Unwin, 1970. (1. edn. 1933).

Bloomfield, L. Literate and illiterate speech. In D. Hymes (ed.), *Language in Culture and Society*. New York: Harper & Row, 1964, pp. 391–396. (Originally published 1927.)

Blumenthal, A. L. *Language and Psychology*. New York: Wiley & Sons, 1970.

Blumenthal, A. L. Psychology and linguistics. The first half-century. In S. Koch and D. E. Leary (eds.), *A Century of Psychology as Science*. New York: McGraw-Hill, 1985, pp. 804–824.

Bohr, N. Analysis and synthesis in science. In O. Neurath, R. Carnap, and C. Morris (eds.), *Foundations of the Unity of Science. International Encyclopedia of Unified Science*, Vol. **1**, No. 1, 1938, p. 28.

Boring, E. G. *A History of Experimental Psychology*. (2nd edn.) New York: Appleton-Century-Crofts, 1950.

Brown, R. *Words and Things*. New York: Free Press, 1958.

Brown, R. *A First Language. The Early Stages*. London: Allen & Unwin, 1973.

Bruner, J. *Child's Talk. Learning to Use Language*. Oxford: Oxford University Press, 1983.

Bühler, K. *Sprachtheorie. Die Darstellungsfunktion der Sprache*. Stuttgart: Fischer, 1978. (Originally published 1934.)

Burling, R. *Man's many Voices: Language in Its Cultural Context*. New York: Holt, Rinehart & Winston, 1970.

Campbell, N. *What is Science*. New York: Dover, 1953. (1. edn. 1921.)

Carroll, J. B. Psychology and linguistics. Detachment and affiliation in the second half-century. In S. Koch and D. E. Leary (eds.), *A Century of Psychology as Science*. New York: McGraw-Hill, 1985, pp. 825–854.

Cassirer, E. *An Essay on Man: An Introduction to a Philosophy of Human Culture*. New Haven: Yale University Press, 1944.

Chalmers, A. F. *What is this Thing Called Science?* (2nd edn.) The open University Press, 1982.

Chomsky, N. *Syntactic Structures*. The Hague: Mouton, 1957.

Chomsky, N. Verbal behavior. By B. F. Skinner. *Language*, 1959, **35**, 26–58.

Chomsky, N. *Language and Mind*. (Enlarged edn.) New York: Harcourt, Brace & Jovanovich, 1972.

Chomsky, N. *Rules and Representations*. Oxford: Blackwell, 1980. (American edn. New York: Columbia University Press, 1979).

Clark, H. H. and Clark, E. V. *Psychology and Language. An Introduction to Psycholinguistics*. New York: Harcourt, Brace & Jovanovich, 1977.

Culler, J. *Saussure*. Glasgow: Collins Sons, 1976.

Dummett, M., Frege, Gottlob. In P. Edwards (ed.), *The Encyclopedia of Philosophy*, **3**, New York: Macmillan, 1967, pp. 225–237.

Dummett, M. *The Interpretation of Frege's Philosophy*. London: Duckworth, 1981.

Ervin-Tripp, S. Imitation and structural change in children's language. In E. H. Lenneberg (ed.), *New Directions in the Study of Language*. Cambridge, Mass.: M.I.T. Press, 1964, pp. 163–189.

Feyerabend, P. *Aagainst Method. Outline of an Anarchistic Theory of Knowledge*. London: Verso, 1975.

Findlay, J. N. Hegel. In D. J. O'Connor (ed.), *A Critical History of Western Philosophy*. New York: Free Press, 1964.

Fodor, J. A. *The Language of Thought*. New York: Crowell, 1975.

Frege, G. On sense and reference. In P. Geach and M. Black (eds.), *Translations from the Philosophical Writings of Gottlob Frege*. Oxford: Blackwell, 1977, pp. 56–78. (Originally published 1892.)

Frege, G. On concept and object. In P. Geach and M. Black (eds.), *Translations from the Philosophical Writings of Gottlob Frege*. Oxford: Blackwell, 1977, pp. 42–55. (Originally published 1892.)

Fromkin, V. and Rodman, R. *An Introduction to Language*. (3rd edn.) New York: Holt, Rinehart & Winston, 1983.

Gardner, B. T. and Gardner, R. A. Two-way communication with an infant chimpanzee. In A. M. Schrier and F. Stollnitz (eds.), *Behaviour in Nonhuman Primates*, Vol. **4**. New York: Academic Press, 1971, pp. 117–184.

Geschwind, N. Specializations of the Human Brain. In *The Brain. A Scientific American Book*. San Fransisco: Freeman, 1979, pp. 108–117.
Glass, A. L. and Holyoak, K. J. *Cognition*. (2nd edn.) New York: Random House, 1986.
Gleitman, L. R. and Wanner, E. Language acquisition: the state of the state of the art. In E. Wanner and L. R. Gleitman (eds.), *Language Acquisition. The State of the Art*. Cambridge: Cambridge University Press, 1982, pp. 3–48.
Goodman, N. *The Structure of Appearance*. Cambridge, Mass.: Harvard University Press, 1951.
Goodglass, H. Is model building advancing neurolinguistics? *The Behavioral and Brain Sciences*, **2**, 1979, p. 466.
Greenberg, J. H. Some universals of grammar with particular reference to the order of meaningful elements. In J. H. Greenberg (ed.), *Universals of Language*. Cambridge, Mass.: M.I.T. Press, 1963, pp. 73–113.
Greenberg, J. H. *Language Universals*. The Hague: Mouton, 1966.
Grice, H. P. Logic and conversation. In P. Cole and J. L. Morgan (eds.), *Syntax and Semantics*, vol. **3**; *Speech Acts*. New York: Academic Press, 1975, pp. 41–58.
Gumperz, H. J. *Discourse Strategies*. Cambridge: Cambridge University Press, 1982.
Halliday, M. A. K. *Explorations in the Functions of Language*. London: Arnold, 1973.
Halliday, M. A. K. *Learning How to Mean*. London: Arnold, 1975.
Hanson, N. R. *Patterns of Discovery*. Cambridge: Cambridge University Press, 1965.
Harnad, S. R. and Steklis, H. D., and Lancaster, J. (eds.), *Origins and Evolution of Language and Speech*. New York: The New York Academy of Sciences, 1976.
Harrè, R. *The Philosophies of Science*. Oxford: Oxford University Press, 1972.
Harris, Z. S. *Structural Linguistics*. Chicago: University of Chicago Press, 1951.
Hegel, G. W. F. *Phenomenologie des Geistes*. Hamburg: Meinier, 1952. (Originally published 1807.)
Hegel, G. W. F. *Wissenschaft der Logic*, **1**, **2**. Frankfurt a. Main: Suhrkamp, 1969. (Originally published 1812.)
Herrnstein, R. J. and Villiers, P. A. de. Fish as a natural category for people and pigeons. *The Psychology of Learning and Motivation*, **14**, 1980, 59–95.
Hewes, G. W. The current status of the gestural theory of language origin. In S. R. Harnad, H. D. Steklis, and J. Lancaster, (eds.), *Origins and Evolution of Language and Speech*. New York: The New York Academy of Sciences, 1976, pp. 482–504.
Hockett, C. F. *A Course in Modern Linguistics*. New York: Macmillan, 1958.
Hörmann, H. *Psychologie der Sprache*. Berlin: Springer, 1970.
Hovdhagen, E. *Foundations of Western Linguistics. From the Beginning to the End of the First Millenium A. D.* Oslo: Oslo University Press, 1982.
Hymes, D. *Foundations in Socio-linguistics. An Ethnographic Approach*. Philadelphia: University of Pennsylvania Press, 1974.
Humboldt, W. von. Über die Verschiedenheit des menschlichen Sprachbaues und ihren Einfluss auf die geistige Entwicklung des Menschengeschlechts. In *Wilhelm von Humboldt Schriften*. München: Goldmann, 1964. (Originally published 1835. Transl. of quote by the present writer.)

Jespersen, O. *Language: Its Nature, Development and Origin.* London: Allen & Unwin, 1922.

Kainz, F. *Psychologie der Sprache.* Vol. **2**. Stuttgart, Enke, 1960.

Kripke, S. A. *Naming and Necessity.* Cambridge: Harvard University Press, 1972.

Kuhn, Th. S. *The Structure of Scientific Revolutions.* (2nd enlarged edn.) Chicago: The University of Chicago Press, 1970. (1. edn. 1962.)

Labov, W. The notion of 'system' in Creole studies. In D. Hymes (ed.), *Pidginization and Creolization of Languages.* Cambridge: Cambridge University Press, 1971, pp. 447–472.

Langacker, R. W. *Language and its Structure.* New York: Harcourt, Brace & World, 1967.

Leakey, R. E. *The Making of Mankind.* New York: Dutton, 1981.

Lenneberg, E. H. *Biological Foundations of Language.* New York: Wiley, 1967.

Levitin, K. *One is not Born a Personality. Profiles of Soviet Education Psychologists* (transl. from the Russian by Yevgeni Filippov). Moscow: Progress Publishers, 1982.

Limber, J. Language in child and chimp. In Th. A. Sebeok and J. Umiker-Sebeok, (eds.), *Speaking of Apes. A Critical Anthology of Two-Way Communication with Man.* New York: Plenum Press, 1980, pp. 197–220.

Losee, J. *A Historical Introduction to the Philosophy of Science.* Oxford: Oxford University Press, 1980.

Lyons, J. *Introduction to Theoretical Linguistics.* Cambridge: The Cambridge University Press, 1968.

Lyons, J. *Semantics,* **1**, **2**. Cambridge: The Cambridge University Press, 1977.

Lyons, J. *Language and Linguistics. An Introduction.* Cambridge: Cambridge University Press, 1981.

Macnamara, J. *Names for Things. A Study of Human Learning.* Cambridge: M.I.T. Press, 1982.

Malinowski, B. The problem of meaning in primitive languages. In C. K. Ogden and J. A. Richards (eds.), *The Meaning of Meaning.* London: Routledge & Kegan Paul, 1972, pp. 296–336. (Originally published 1923.)

Marler, P. The evolution of communication: affect or cognition? In K. R. Scherer and P. Ekman (eds.), *Approaches to Emotion.* Hilsdale, N. J.: Erlbaum, 1984, pp. 345–365.

Marler, P. The evolution of communication. In T. Sebeok (ed.), *How Animals Communicate.* Bloomington: Indiana University Press, 1977, pp. 45–70.

Marler, P. and Green, S. The analysis of animal communication. In P. Marler and J. G. Vandenbergh (eds.), *Handbook of Behavioral Neurobiology.* Vol. **3**. *Social Behavior and Communication.* New York: Plenum Press, 1979, pp. 73–158.

Matthews, P. H. *Inflectional Morphology. A Theoretical Study Based on Aspects of Latin Verb Conjugation.* Cambridge: Cambridge University Press, 1972.

Mayr, E. *The Growth of Biological Thought.* Cambridge: Mass.: Harvard University Press, 1982.

Mead, G. H. *Mind, Self, and Society*. Chicago: University of Chicago Press, 1962. (Originally published 1934.)

Mill, J. S. *A System of Logic*. London: Longmans, Green & Co., 1956. (Originally published 1843.)

Miller, G. A. and Johnson-Laird, P. N. *Language and Perception*. Cambridge, Mass.: Harvard University Press, 1976.

Morris, C. *Science, Language, and Behavior*. New York: Prentice-Hall, 1946.

Mounin, G. Language, communication, chimpanzees. In Th. A. Sebeok and J. Umiker-Sebeok (eds.), *Speaking of Apes. A Critical Anthology of Two-way Communication with Man*. New York: The Plenum Press, 1980, pp. 161–177.

Mowrer, O. *Learning Theory and the Symbolic Processes*. New York: Wiley, 1966. pp. 14–50.

Osgood, C. E. *Method and Theory in Experimental Psychology*. New York: Oxford University Press, 1953.

Osgood, C. E. and Sebeok, Th. A. (eds.), *Psycholonguistics: A Survey of Theory and Research Problems*. Bloomington: Indiana University Press, 1965.

Paivio, A. and Begg, I. *Psychology and Language*. Englewood Cliffs, N. J.: Prentice-Hall, 1981.

Passingham, R. *The Human Primate*. Oxford: Freeman, 1982.

Paul, H. *Prinzipien der Sprachgeschichte*. (5 edn.) Tübingen: Niemeyer, 1920. (1. edn. 1880.)

Piaget, J. *The Language and Thought of the Child*. London: Routledge & Kegan Paul, 1959. (Originally published 1926.)

Piaget, J. *The Psychology of Intelligence*. London: Routledge & Kegan, Paul 1950.

Piaget, J. and Inhelder, B. *The Psychology of the Child*. London: Routledge & Kegan Paul, 1969.

Popper, K. R. *The Logic of Scientific Discovery*. New York: Harper & Row, 1959. (Originally published 1934.)

Popper, K. R. *Conjectures and Refutations. The Growth of Scientific Knowledge*. London: Routledge & Kegan Paul, 1963.

Posner, M. I. and Keele, S. W. On the genesis of abstract ideas. *The Journal of Experimental Psychology*, **77**, 1968, 353–363.

Premack, D. On the assessment of language competence in the chimpanzee. In A. M. Schrier and F. Stollnitz (eds.), *Behaviour of Nonhuman Primates*. Vol. **4**. New York: Academic Press, 1971, pp. 185–228.

Premack, D. *Gavagai! or the Future History of the Animal Language Controversy*. Cambridge: Mass., M.I.T. Press, 1986.

Putnam, H. Is semantics possible? In Putnam, *Mind, Language, and Reality. Philosophical Papers*, Vol. **2**. Cambridge, Mass.: Cambridge University Press, 1973, pp. 139 –152.

Quine, W. V. Natural kinds. In S. P. Schwartz (ed.), *Naming, Necessity, and Natural Kinds*. Itacha: Cornell University Press, 1977, pp. 155–175.

Quine, W. O. *Word and Object*. Cambridge: M.I.T. Press, 1960.

Reinvang, I. *Aphasia and Brain Organization*. New York: Plenum Press, 1985.

Robins, R. H. *A Short History of Linguistics*. (2nd edn.) New York: Longman, 1979.
Rosch, E. Principles of categorization. In E. Rosch and B. B. Lloyd (eds.), *Cognition and Categorization*. Hillsdale, N. J.: Erlbaum, 1978, pp. 27–47.
Russel, B. *Logic and Knowledge. Essays 1901–1950*. (Edit. by R. C. March) London: Allen & Unwin, 1956.
Ryle, G. *The Concept of Mind*. Harmondsworth: Penguin Books, 1949.
Ryle, G. The theory of meaning. In C. A. Mace (ed.), *British Philosophy in the Mid-Century. A Cambridge Symposium*. London: Allen & Unwin, 1957.
Sapir, E. *Language. An Introduction to the Study of Speech*. New York: Harcourt, Brace & World, 1949. (Originally published 1921.)
Saugstad, P. Problem solving as dependent on availability of functions. *British Journal of Psychology*, 1955, **46**, 191–198.
Saugstad, P. *An Inquiry into the Foundations of Psychology*. Oslo: Universitetsforlaget, 1965.
Saugstad, P. *A Theory of Communication and Use of Language. Foundations for the Study of Psychology*. Oslo: Universitetsforlaget, 1977.
Saugstad, P. *A Theory of Language and Understanding*. Oslo: Universitetsforlaget, 1980.
Saugstad, P.: Towards a Methodology for the Study of Psychology. In I. Bjørgen (ed.), *Problems in Psychology: A Scandinavian Contribution*. Bergen and London: Sigma 1989.
Saussure, F. de *Course in General Linguistics*. (translated by W. Baskin). London: Owen, 1960. (Originally published 1918.)
Savage-Rumbaugh, E. S., Rumbaugh, D. M., and Boysen, S. Linguistically mediated tool use and exchange by chimpanzees. (*Pan troglodytes*). In Th. A. Sebeok and J. Umiker-Sebeok (eds.), *Speaking of Apes: A Critical Anthology of Two-Way Communication with Man*. New York: Plenum Press, 1980, pp. 353–384.
Savage-Rumbaugh, E. S. *Pan paniscus* and *Pan troglodytes*. Contrasts in preverbal communicative competence. In R. L. Susman (ed.), *The Pygmy Chimpanzee*. New York: Plenum Press, 1984, pp. 395–413.
Savage-Rumbaugh, S., Rumbaugh, D. M., and McDonald, K. Language learning in two species of apes. *Neuroscience and Biobehavioural Reviews*, **9**, 1985, 653–665.
Savage-Rumbaugh, E. S., Sevcik, R. A., Rumbaugh, D. M., and Rubert, E. The capacity of animals to acquire language: do species differences have anything to say us? *Philosophical Transactions Royal Society London*, 1985, **B. 308**, 177–185.
Savage-Rumbaugh, S., McDonald, K., Sevcik, R. A., Hopkins, W. D., and Rubert, E. Spontaneous symbol acquisition and communicative use by pygmy chimpanzees (*Pan paniscus*). *Journal of Experimental Psychology: General*, 1986, **115**, 211–235.
Schank, R. C. Process models and language. *The Behavioral and Brain Sciences*, **2**, 1979, 474–475.
Scharf, J.-H. (ed.) Evolution. *Nova Acta Leopoldina*, **42**, 1975.
Schwartz, S. P. Introduction. In S. P. Schwartz (ed.), *Naming, Necessity, and Naturual Kinds*. Itacha: Cornell University Press, 1977.
Searle, J. R. Proper names and descriptions. In E. Edwards (ed.), *The Encyclopedia of Philosophy*, **6**, New York: Macmillan, 1967, pp. 487–491.

Shapere, D. Scientific Theories and their domains. In F. Suppe (ed.), *The Structure of Scientific Theories*. (2nd edn.) Urbana: Illini Book Edition, 1977, pp. 518–599.

Skinner, B. F. *Verbal Behavior*. New York: Appleton-Century-Crofts, 1957.

Sternberg, R. J. (ed.), *Handbook of Intelligence*. Cambridge: Cambridge University Press, 1982.

Strawson, P. F. Review of Wittgenstein's *Philosophical Investigations*. *Mind*, **63**, 1954, 70–99.

Suppe, F. The search for philosophical understanding of scientific theories. In F. Suppe (ed.), *The Structure of Scientific Theories*. (2nd edn.) Urbana: Illini Book Edition, 1977, pp. 3–241.

Suppe, F. Afterword–1977. In F. Suppe (ed.), *The Structure of Scientific Theories*. (2nd edn.) Urbana: Illini Book Edition, 1977, pp. 617–730.

Terrace, H. S. In the beginning was the "name". *American Psychologist*, 1985, **40**, Sept. (9), 1011–1028.

Tolman, E. C. *Purpose Behavior in Animals and Men*. Berkeley: The University of California, 1932.

Tolman, E. C. Cognitive maps in rats and men. *The Psychological Review*, **55**, 1948, 189–209.

Toulmin, S. *Foresight and Understanding*. New York: Harper & Row, 1963.

Umiker-Sebeok, J. and Sebeok, Th. A. Introduction: Questioning apes. In Th. A. Sebeok and J. Umiker-Sebeok (eds.), *Speaking of Apes: A critical anthology of Two-Way Communication with Man*. New York: Plenum Press, 1980, pp. 1–60.

Vygotsky, L. S. *Thought and Language*. (Edit. and transl. by E. Hanfmann and G. Vakar.) Cambridge: M.I.T. Press, 1962. (Originally published 1934.)

Vygotsky, L. S. *Mind in Society. The Development of Higher Psychological Processes*. In M. Cole, V. John-Steiner, S. Scribner, and E. Souberman (eds.). Cambridge: Harvard University Press, 1978.

Washburn, S. L. Primate field studies and social science. In L. Nader and Th. W. Maretzsky (eds.), *Cultural Illness and Health. Anthropological Studies*, **9**, 1973, 128–134.

Washburn, S. L. and McCown, E. R. Human evolution and social science. In S. L. Washburn and E. R. McCown (eds.), *Human Evolution. Biosocial Perspectives*. Menlo Park, Cal.: Benjamin/Cummings, 1978, pp. 285–295.

Washburn, S. L. and Strum, S. C. Concluding comments. In S. L. Washburn and P. Dolhinow (eds.), *Perspectives on Human Evolution*, **2**. New York: Holt, Rinehart & Winston, 1972, pp. 469–491.

Wittgenstein, L. *Logisch-philosophische Abhandlung*. *Annalen der Naturphilosophie*, 1921.

Wittgenstein, L. *Philosophical Investigations*. (Transl. by G. E. M. Anscombe.) Oxford: Blackwell, 1953.

Woozley, D. D. Universals. In P. Edwards (ed.), *The Encyclopedia of Philosophhy*, **8**. New York: Macmillan, 1967, pp. 194–206.

Wundt, W. *Völkerpsychologie. Die Sprache*, **1**, **2**. Leipzig: Engelmann, 1911, 1912. (Originally published 1900.)

Index of Autors

Alston, W. P., 27
Antsiferova, L. J., Author's Preface
Arbib, M. A., 34
Aristotle, 83, 86
Augustine, 45, 66
Austin, J. L., 45, 58, 98, 124
Ayer, A., 45

Badrian, A., 135
Badrian, N., 135
Barth, F., Author's Preface
Barwise, J., 29, 50, 55, 113, 115
Bates, E., 122
Bateson, G., 93
Begg, I., 55
Berkeley, G., 86, 90
Berlin, B., 32
Bickerton, D., 14, 62
Bloom, L., 33
Bloomfield, L., 9, 14, 17, 24, 28, 71
Blumenthal, A. L., 25, 33
Boas, F., 9, 23
Bohr, N., 7
Boring, E. G., 86
Brentano, F., 44
Broca, P., 33, 34, 35, 134–135
Brown, R., 33
Bruner, J., 128
Brushlinsky, A. W., Author's Preface
Burling, R., 25
Bühler, K., 26, 27, 32

Campell, N., 75
Caplan, D., 34
Carnap, R., 45
Carroll, J. B., 33
Cassirer, E., 27
Chalmers, A. F., 68, 71
Chomsky, N., 10–13, 14, 17, 26, 29, 30, 32, 35, 40, 49, 50, 62, 65, 71, 121, 123, 131
Clark, E. V., 30, 32, 33, 98, 101, 114, 116, 137, 140
Clark, H. H., 30, 32, 33, 98, 101, 114, 116, 137, 140
Culler, J., 11

Dahl, R., Author's Preface
Darwin, C., 36, 53, 75
Davidson, D., 45
Descartes, R., 44, 83, 90
Dummett, M., 45, 49, 83
Døving, K., Author's Preface

Elgmork, K., Author's Preface
Endresen, R. T., Author's Preface
Erwin-Tripp, S., 140

Feyerabend, P., 69
Findley, J. N., 86
Fodor, J. A., 62, 109
Frege, G., 44, 58, 83, 106, 108
Fromkin, V., 8, 16

Gardner, B. T., 38
Gardner, R. A., 38
Geschwind, N., 33, 34, 134
Glass, A. L., Author's Preface, 30, 33, 35
Glefjeld, R., Author's Preface
Gleitman, L. R., 70
Goodglass, H., 34
Goodman, N., 28
Green, S., 59
Greenberg, J. H., 17
Grice, H. P., 114
Gumperz, J. J., 23, 127

Halliday, M. A. K., 139
Hanson, N. R., 69
Harnad, S. R., 40
Harré, R., 70
Harris, Z. S., 17
Hegel, G. W. F., 86
Helmholtz, H. von, 86
Helstrup, T., Author's Preface

Herbart, F., 26
Herder, J., 10, 20, 44, 49
Hering, E., 86
Herrnstein, R. J., 86
Hewes, G. W., 133
Hockett, C. F., 122
Holyoak, K. J., 30, 33, 35
Hovdhaugen, E., Author's Preface, 8
Humboldt, W. von, 10, 20, 26, 31, 44, 49
Hume, D., 86, 90, 91, 93
Husserl, E., 44, 50
Hymes, D., 23, 24, 40, 62, 127, 135, 137
Hörmann, H., 27

Inhelder, B., 139

Jakobson, R., 17, 27
Jespersen, O., 8
Johnson-Laird, P. N., 19, 32, 83
Jones, W., 8

Kainz, F., 27
Kaiser, M., Author's Preface
Kanner, L., 138
Kay, P., 32
Keele, S. W., 93
Kerry, B., 44
Kripke, S. A., 97, 106
Kuhn, Th. S., 69, 74

Labov, W., 10, 19
Lancaster, J., 40
Langacker, R. W., 24
Leakey, R. E., 24
Lenneberg, E. H., 34, 37, 62, 139
Levitin, K., 54
Lian, A., Author's Preface
Limber, J., 134
Lindeman, F. O., Author's Preface
Locke, J., 44, 86, 90
Lomov, B. F., Author's Preface
Losee, J., 75
Lyons, J., 8, 12, 13, 14, 16, 18, 19, 28, 98, 108, 109, 122
Løvlie, A., Author's Preface

Mach, E., 68
Macnamara, J., 55, 137, 138, 139
MacWinney, B., 122
Malinowski, B., 57, 62
Marler, P., Author's Preface, 47, 59, 62
McCown, E. R., 36
Matthews, P. H., 16
Mayr, E., 43
Mead, G. H., 53, 113, 114
Mill, J. S., 106
Miller, G. A., 19, 32, 83
Morris, C., 28
Mounin, G., 11
Mowrer, G., 27, 60

Osgood, C. E., 27, 60

Paivio, A., 55
Palm, E., Author's Preface
Passingham, R., 23, 36, 47
Paul, H., 8, 26
Perry, J., 29, 50, 55, 113, 115
Piaget, J., 26, 30, 44, 58, 137, 139
Plato, 86
Popper, K. R., 68, 77
Posner, M. I., 93
Premack, D., 38, 140
Price, H. H., 91
Putnam, H., 97, 98

Quine, W. O., 28, 45, 50

Reinvang, Y., 34
Robins, R. H., 8, 10, 18, 25
Rodman, R., 8, 16
Rosch, E., 32, 93, 98
Russell, B., 58, 90, 91, 93
Ryle, G., 45, 98
Raaheim, K., Author's Preface

Sapir, E., 9, 10, 17, 23, 44, 49
Saugstad, P., 28, 31, 40, 50, 55, 74, 75, 93, 115, 116, 135, 140
Saussure, F., 9, 10–13, 20, 23, 24, 31, 32, 35, 44, 49, 81, 130
Savage-Rumbaugh, E. S., 38, 39, 135
Schank, R. C., 30
Scharf, J.-H., 40
Schlick, M., 45
Schwartz, S. P., 98
Searle, J. R., 106
Sebeok, Th. A., 27, 38

Shapere, D., 69, 72–73
Skinner, B. F., 27, 50, 60
Steklis, H. D., 40
Sternberg, R. J., 30, 52
Stinessen, L., Author's Preface
Strawson, P. F., 109
Strum, S. C., 36, 47, 59, 62
Sundal, K. M., Author's Preface
Suppe, F., 67, 69, 71, 72, 76

Terrace, H. S., 38
Tolman, E. C., 29, 113
Toulmin, S., 69, 73, 75
Trubetzkoy, N., 17, 26

Umiker-Sebeok, J., 38

Villiers, P. A. de, 86
Vygotsky, L. S., 27, 32, 54, 57, 130

Wallace, A. R., 75
Wang, W. S.-J. Author's Preface
Wanner, E., 70
Washburn, S. L., Author's Preface, 36, 38, 47, 59, 62
Watson, J. B., 27
Wernicke, C., 33, 34, 35
Whorf, B., 10, 44, 49, 62
Wittgenstein, L., 28, 45, 58, 98, 107, 108, 109, 129
Woozley, D. D., 86, 90, 91
Wright, G. H. von, Author's Preface
Wundt, W., 25, 26, 53

Index of subjects

Analytical philosophy, 44–45, 49, 98
Attention, 61, 51, 62, 116
Animal communication, 36–40, Chapter 3
  Teaching verbal communication to apes, 37–40, Chapter 3, 134, 135
Aphasia and the speech areas, 33–35, 45–46, 134–135
Broca's aphasia
  See Aphasia
Autism, Kanner's, 138
Category, Chapter 5, 102–103
Cognition, 30, 52, 94–95, 97, 130
Communication
  See Language and communication
Comment
  See Topic and comment
Competence and performance, 13, 30, 131
Communicative competence, 23, 40, 127
  See also Skill in use of language
Comprehension and production of speech, 40, 140
Concept, 52–53, Chapter 5, 108–109
Consciousness, 30, 50–53, 90
Creole language, 19
Culture
  See Language and culture
Extension and intension, 98
Fact, 72–73, 77–80
Family resemblance, 98
Grammar, 13, 17, 117, 124–127, 131, 134
  The Study of, 124–127
  See also Sentence
Grammatical rules, 12, 13, 18, 30, 50, 60, 62, 81–82, 127, 136
Historical-comparative study of language, 7, 8–9, 24
Individual differences in use of language, 24–25, 78, 82, 127, 133
Information, the concept, 52, 62, 63, 64, 81, 93, 108, 115–116, 121
  See also Knowledge
Information processing approach, 29–30, 44, 49, 52
Intelligence, 52
Item of information, 72–75, 129
Knowledge
  availability of knowledge, 40, 115–117
  common knowledge, Chapter 5, 113
  differences of knowledge, 81, 113, 135
  its structure, 81, 82, 94–97
  See also Information
La langue and la parole, 12, 131
Language
  and behavior, 6, 27–31, 50, Chapter 3, 77, Chapter 7
  and communication, 6, 23–25, Chapter 3, Chapter 7
  and culture, 23–25
  and emotion, 47, 62–63
  and perception, 32, 36, 78, 81, Chapter 5 and 6
  and thinking, 6, 10, 32, 35, Chapter 2, 46–50, 58–59, 62, 78, 130
  as an instrument, 80–82, 107, 110
  as a system, 10–14, 17–22, 39, 60, 110
  its functions, 6, 23–24, Chapt. 3, 79–82, 117–119, Chapt. 7, 131
  its ontogenesis, 33, 37, 78, 136–140
  its phylogenesis, 36–37, 40, 46–50, 59–63, 133–135
  its social nature, 23–24, 59, 113–115, 135, 138
  its structure, 81–82, Chapter 6, 110–111
Linguistic sign, 16, 80, 82, 110, 126
  See also Morpheme; Word
Linguistic universal, 14–17
Linguistics, 7, 9–22, 24
Lexeme, 15, 80
Logic, 83–84, 91, 97, 98, 106
Material object, 84, 87–88, 89, 90

Meaning, 28–29, 84–85, Chapters 5, 6 and 7
See also Name; Reference; Stimulus; Unit of meaning
Metaphor, 109, 132
Metaphysical belief, role of in science, 70–71, 83–84
Model, use of in scientific research, 32, 82, 129–130
Morpheme, 14, 15–16, 80
Morphology, 125–127, 132
Name, 60, Chapter 6, 134, 139
common name, 103–105
proper name, 105–106
Naming, 37, 38
Noun phrase and verb phrase 15, 123
Particular, the and the universal, Chapter 5
Perception, 47, Chapter 5
See also Language and perception
Performance
See speaker and listener
Competence and reformance
Phatic communion, 57–59, 63
Phenomenology, 30, 83–84, 86–87
Phoneme, 14, 110
Phonology, 12, 17, 21, 133
Polysemy, 109, 132
Positivism, 67–72
Predicate
See Subject and predicate
Private language thesis, 109–110
Proper name
Se Name
Prototype, 93–94
Psycho-linguistics, 25–31
Pure particular, 90–91
Quantification, 76
Reference, Chapter 6
See also Meaning
Resemblance, 91–94
Semantics, 18, 55, 85, 108
Sentence, 11, 13, 14, 15, 22, 32, 40–41, 82, 107, 120–124
See also Grammar
Skill in use of language, 40, 41, 119, 127–128
See also Communicative competence
Speech act, 114, 124
Speech area
See aphasia
Speech community, 24, 62, 135
Speaker and listener
their relationship, 81, 113–115
performance of the speaker, 117–120
performance of the listener, 117–120
Stimulus, the concept, 28–29, 115
Structure and function, 21–22, 23–24, 79–80, 127
See also Language, its structure; its functions
Structuralism, 20–21
Subject and predicate, 122, 125
Syntax, 17, 125–127, 125
System
See Language, as a system
Thinking, Chapter 2
Thinking and language
See Language and thinking
Tool
See Language as an instrument
Topic and comment, 122
Unit of information, 81, 120–124, 132
See Sentence
Unit of meaning, 120, 132
See Word
Universal, the
See Particular, the and the universal
Verb phrase
See Noun phrase and verb phrase
Vocabulary, 12, 60, 111, 117, 134, 138, 139–140
Wernicke's aphasia
See Aphasia
Word, 11–12, 14, 15–16, 131
as an instrument, 110–111
definition of, 15–16, 110
its structure, 110
word conceived of as a linguistic unit, 11–12, 32, 120, 132